RAGING HORMONES

**Martha Williamson
& Robin Sheets**

DOUBLEDAY
New York ▲ London ▲ Toronto
▲ Sydney ▲ Auckland

PUBLISHED BY DOUBLEDAY

a division of Bantam Doubleday Dell
Publishing Group, Inc.
666 Fifth Avenue, New York, New York 10103

DOUBLEDAY and the portrayal of an anchor
with a dolphin are trademarks of
Doubleday,
a division of Bantam Doubleday Dell
Publishing Group, Inc.

Library of Congress
Applied for

ISBN 0-385-26486-0
Printed in the United States of America
March 1990
FIRST EDITION

Authors' Note

• • • • • • • • • • • •
_____

   Some say there is nothing funny about PMS. We say that if
we don't laugh, we'll cry. We have written *Raging Hormones*
because PMS—premenstrual syndrome—has wreaked havoc with
our health, our work, our mental faculties, and our relationships,
not to mention our sense of fashion.

   Up to ninety percent of all women experience some degree of
premenstrual syndrome. PMS is not new. It is not the "Female
Disorder of the Month." Ever since there have been women,
there has been PMS, and it has played a major role in promoting
the destructive image of women as fickle, erratic, moody, un-
predictable, and unreliable.

   Some will say that a humorous book about PMS will set women
back a hundred years. We say that no one can ever move forward
without confronting and controlling the obstacles that threaten
to impede her progress.

   And, we say that sometimes the best way to start taking something seriously is with a sense of humor. We may mock the
syndrome and its symptoms, but never the women who struggle
with them.

Martha Williamson
Robin Sheets

Acknowledgments

• • • • • • • • • • • • •

The authors gratefully acknowledge the following individuals for their contributions to *Raging Hormones.*

Ned Gill, *for the title*
Loretta Barrett
Susan Grode
Richard Garzilli
Skip Adams
Rolfe Arnhym
Francoise Becker, M.S.
Bob Colleary
Billy Delbert
Greg Dix
Dr. Jack Hattem
Dr. Maga Jackson
Kathy Lette
Bill McCall and Kristen McCall
Gordon McKee
Dr. Gwen Nichols
Dr. James Oliver
Dr. John Sheets
Dr. Megan Shields
Dr. Carol Visser
The Good Earth, DeLacey's Club 41, *and other Pasadena restaurants who kept our water glasses filled while we wrote*

CONTENTS

1

Now Is the Winter of Our PMS

What Is a Hormone Hostage? 10

Trudy's Story 11

Easy Quiz #1—Are You a
Hormone Hostage? 12

Real Women Do Get PMS 15

The Hormone Hostage Hall
of Fame 16

2

You're Not Less of a Woman, Just Less of a Human Being

Gwen's Story 17

Things That Do *Not*
Cause PMS 18

Things That Will *Not* Cure
PMS 18

Welcome to the Wild and
Wacky World of PMS 19

Easy Quiz #2—How to Tell
PMS from Your Own
Stupid Character Flaws 20

3

Your Body, Yourself, Your Problem

Dierdre's Story 22

The Bent Neck-Huge Purse
Theory 24

The Hormone Hostage
Cavalcade of Monthly
Complaints: My Monthly
Cycle-Minder 26

Field Guide to the Hormone
Hostage 28

The Seven Warning Signs of
the Questionable Medical
Professional 29

Aerobics and Death 30

The Hormone Hostage
Amazing Chocolate-
and-Salt Diet 32

Easy Quiz #3—What's Your
PMS-IQ? 34

4

Taking It to the Streets

Lana's Story 36

Days o' Death 37

PMS and the Decision-
Making Process 38

Good Reading Material When
You're Trying Not to Eat,
Cry, or Maim Something 39

Do Not Read These Things 39

Your Bed, Your Best Friend 40

Twenty Things the Hormone
Hostage Should Avoid
Completely 41

Celluloid Hell 41

Seize the Day Before It
Seizes You 42

Easy Quiz #4—Should You
Remain Prone? 42

5

The Holistic Hormone Hostage

Hope for Every Hostage 44

Rachel's Story 45

Alternative Therapies 46

Self-Expression 48

Hostage Haiku 48

Ode to Mrs. Fields 49

A Song to Jason 50

One Woman's Road 52

Easy Quiz #5—"I Ovulate,
Therefore I Am" 55

6

The Hormone Hostage in Society

Patience's Story 56

Landmarks in PMS History 58

Should a Woman
Be President? 65

Little-Known Facts
About PMS 66

Easy Quiz #6—Hostage
on a Hot Tin Roof 67

7

PMS Is Everybody's Business

Jackie's Story 68

The Hormone Hostage
on the Job 69

Do's and Don'ts in the
Premenstrual Workplace 69

Jobs Just for You 70

Hormone Hostages Need Not
Apply 70

Easy Quiz #7—The
Williamson-Sheets
Personality Profile
to Determine
Employment Suitability 71

8

A Hormone Is a Terrible Thing to Waste

Debbie's Story 73

Debbie Does the Mall 74

Copping a Premenstrual Plea 76

Contents 7

Assault with a Deadly
Hormone 77

I Want to Live, but Not
Right Now 78

The Mind of the Hormone
Hostage 79

The Gullibility Factor 80

Easy Quiz #8—Beyond the
Subconscious Hormone 81

9

Women Who Love Men Who Hate Women with PMS

Pat's Story 82

A Slip of the Lip Can Sink
a Relationship! 84

Hormone Heroes 85

Remember Eva Braun 85

The Walking Wounded 86

Advice to Hearts and
Hormones 87

When You Care Enough
to Send the PMS 88

Easy Quiz #9—Love Me,
Love My Hormones 90

10

The Hormone Hostage Homemaker from Hell

Phyllis' Story 92

Hostage Homemaker Handy
Hints 93

Children of a Lesser Mother 95

Why Mommy Can't Read 96

Snow White 96

Other Domestic Fables for
Our Time 97

That Was No Lady, That
Was My Mother 98

Easy Quiz #10—Home Is
Where Your Hormones
Are 99

11

The Hormone Hostage on Campus

Courtney's Story 100

Don'ts for the Campus
Hostage 102

Phi Mu Sigma 103

Easy Quiz #11—Taking
the PMAT—"The
Premenstrual Aptitude
Test" 107

12

The Hormone Hostage on Her Own

Donna's Story 109

Single but Not Alone 110

I've Got a Right to Scream
the Blues   110

Caveats for the Unmarried
PMS Victim   111

Full Refrigerator and Empty
Arms   112

Tracking the Perfect PMS
Mate   112

Looking for Love in All the
Right Professions   113

Easy Quiz #12—"Are You
Better Off Single?"   113

Hormone Hostage on Board! 120

Hormone Hostage
International   121

Hormone Hostage Alert ID
Bracelet   122

Suggested Reading   123

The Hostage's Creed   124

Bibliography   125

About the Authors 126

13

PMS and Proud

Gloria's Story   115
We Are Not Alone   116
Hostages Helping Hostages   117

PMS \pee-em-ess\ *n* [ME, fr. MF & LL]: PREMENSTRUAL SYNDROME **1**: female monthly malady with symptoms of varying degrees of physical discomfort, emotional upheaval, depression, and erratic behavior **2**: mood swings, inexplicable acts; precipitates/may occur in conjunction with a woman's menses *syn* see BITCH, HELLHAG, HORMONE HOSTAGE . . .

1
NOW IS THE WINTER OF OUR PMS

In which we are introduced to PMS—what it is and what it isn't. This chapter will NOT contain the phrase "A Celebration of Woman."

• • • • • • • • • • • •

What Is a Hormone Hostage?

HORMONE HOSTAGE: Any Woman Who for Two to Fourteen Days Each Month Becomes a Prisoner of Her Own **"Raging Hormones"** and Plummets Her Life and the Lives of Those Around Her into an Unholy Premenstrual Netherworld.

In the next fifteen seconds, another woman will pass from postmenstrual to premenstrual. The monthly battle of the hormones will begin, and the days between ovulation and menstruation will launch a hormonal civil war. Her body will become a police state and her mind will once again be missing in action. Finally, menstruation brings a blessed truce . . . until next month.

Is premenstrual syndrome the real thing or just propaganda? Everybody knows PMS is just an excuse to leave work early or get an extension on your English paper or cancel that dinner party, right? It's all in your mind, right? You buy ten doughnuts once a month and eat them all before you get to your car because you *want* to, right?

Come on. Think about it. Premenstrual syndrome isn't just an excuse for your fat ankles and irrational behavior. Maybe it's the *reason*.

Are you willing to remain a monthly hostage in the menstrual wars?

Are you willing to enter the demilitarized zone and take responsibility for your hormones?

Are you willing to accept that there is no lasting peace unless you are pregnant, dead, or over fifty?

PMS fights dirty. All you can do is counterattack one month at a time—a little yoga here, a little progesterone there, an occasional deep-breathing exercise, and laying off the Snickers. And if all else fails, you can always scream and break stemware.

Trudy's Story

I used to think I was crazy. I mean, sometimes I'd just start acting like somebody else. One night I had this sudden craving for honey-roasted peanuts. Before I knew it, I was on a plane to Phoenix asking the stewardess for a second bag. Somewhere over Denver I realized things like this had happened before. Like the time my car broke down and I set it on fire to attract a passing motorist. Or the time I cashed in my life insurance to send twelve thousand inner-city children on a tour of Graceland. They seemed to enjoy it and I did get several nice letters, but this wasn't typical behavior for me.

I finally began to notice that I was always disoriented, irritable, and overly sensitive just before I got my period. Could this be more than a coincidence? Could I be a Hormone Hostage?

wwwwwwwwwwwwwwwwwwwwwwwwwwwwwww

Easy Quiz #1
ARE YOU A HORMONE HOSTAGE?

Answer the following questions as honestly as you can. If you find them too personal, too confusing, or too draining, you're probably ovulating. Skip to Chapter Two.

▲ *Part One: Circle the Answer That Most Applies to You*

1. **Three days before your period, you stock up on:**
   a. tampons
   b. chocolate ice cream
   c. hollow-point bullets

2. **Water weight gain forces you to:**
   a. take occasional diuretics
   b. wear maternity clothes
   c. widen the doorways in your home

3. **Monthly depression prevents you from:**
   a. accepting social invitations
   b. leaving your home
   c. interacting with the other patients

4. **The waitress gave you regular coffee instead of decaffeinated. You:**
   a. leave no tip
   b. stay up 'til midnight detailing your car
   c. lie awake wondering who else is out to get you

5. **Three days before your period a single glass of wine will:**
   a. relax you
   b. depress you
   c. cause you to become sexually aroused by glancing at Ed McMahon's picture on a letter from Publishers Clearing House

6. Once a month, you want to:
   a. change your hair
   b. change your job
   c. end your life

7. You are in a department store. Impulsively, you buy:
   a. ten pairs of pantyhose, on sale
   b. ten pairs of sensible shoes, on sale
   c. a blue fox stroller, no payments 'til March

8. You constantly misplace your keys and usually find them:
   a. in a coat pocket
   b. in the freezer
   c. in the ignition with the car running and the doors locked

9. Your secretary neglects to give you an important telephone message. You:
   a. gently reprimand her
   b. demote her to Central Processing
   c. call her a tramp and sleep with her husband

10. The little boy next door has scrawled an obscene word on your garage door. You:
    a. make him sponge it off
    b. make him lick it off
    c. correct his spelling and leave it there

▲ *Part Two: Answer Yes or No*

In the days before your period, do any of the following apply to you?

1. Your pizza needs salt.

2. Friends use your skin to sharpen blunt objects.

3. You begin to carry a diaphragm in your purse.

4. You call in sick because you can't decide what to wear.

5. You bring home a hitchhiker and loan him your car.

6. You experience short-term memory loss.

7. You have a curious inability to distinguish right from wrong.

8. You experience short-term memory loss.

9. You develop an increased intolerance for all forms of carbon-based life.

10. No one understands you and it's just as well as far as you're concerned.

11. The sight of a fireman petting his dog makes you cry.

12. You don't talk when you can point or nod.

K E Y

Part One If you answered "a" to six or more questions, your premenstrual syndrome is mild. Get out of bed and go to work. You have no excuse.

If you answered "b" to six or more questions, chances are you experience some measure of monthly malady. Your PMS is most likely easily managed by diet, exercise, and other therapy. You're going to have to find another excuse for your shoplifting and excessive drinking.

If you answered "c" to six or more questions, don't let this upset you, but the chances are—and it's really not that bad, okay?—that you may very well be . . . well, let's just see how you did on Part Two, all right?

Part Two If you replied no to seven or more of the questions, you clearly fall within established parameters for moderate premenstrual syndrome. It should not seriously interfere with your day-to-day mundane existence.

HOWEVER . . .

If you answered yes to seven or more questions, the good news is that you are most likely perceived by your peers as a very unique though not highly trustworthy individual. You won't have to worry about people asking you to do spur-of-the-moment babysitting.

This does mean, though, that certain facts must be faced. There will be days every month when traffic lights seem complicated, when your gardener looks attractive, when beer commercials make you cry, and when the slightest change in cabin pressure sends you to bed—and you may not even be in a plane. The road you travel is strewn with broken dreams, broken dates, and broken dishes.

Brace yourself, honey:

YOU ARE A HORMONE HOSTAGE

Real Women Do Get PMS

It's okay to be a Hormone Hostage. Recognizing it is the first step to coping with it. Hey, everybody knows somebody with PMS. Why do you think your teacher made everybody take naps . . . in eighth grade? Why do you think the lady next door always parked on your front lawn every four weeks? Remember how you knew your mother was getting her period? She'd put TV dinners in the oven and then forget to turn it on.

Come on. PMS has been around ever since women have been menstruating. Actually, a few days before that. So, if you've got it, you've got it. Admit it or people will just think you took too many drugs in college.

The Hormone Hostage Hall of Fame

Premenstrual syndrome is no respecter of persons. It does not discriminate based on race, nationality, religion, income, or social status. Just sex. Many great women have been Hormone Hostages and many have not. PMS certainly didn't prevent them from making their unique mark on history, but who knows how it affected the kind of mark they made? For example, where would we be if three days before her period, Queen Isabella told Columbus she wanted to go along and steer?

Herewith a comparison of women who may or may not have had PMS.

Probably Not	Bet Your House on It
Shirley Temple Black	Bess Myerson
Florence Griffith Joyner	Mary Decker
Lynn Redgrave	Vanessa Redgrave
Beryl Markham	Amelia Earhart
Corazon Aquino	Imelda Marcos
Tina Turner	Janis Joplin
Shirley MacLaine	Shirley MacLaine
	Shirley MacLaine
	Shirley MacLaine
Harriet Tubman	Mary Todd Lincoln
Katharine Hepburn	Vivien Leigh
Beverly Sills	Maria Callas
The Kennedy Women	The Manson Women
Mother Teresa	Tammy Faye Bakker
Golda Meir	Indira Gandhi
Mamie Eisenhower	Eva Perón
The Lennon Sisters	The Pointer Sisters
Erma Bombeck	Dorothy Parker
Ivana Trump	Leona Helmsley
Oprah Winfrey	Geraldo Rivera

2
YOU'RE NOT LESS OF A WOMAN. JUST LESS OF A HUMAN BEING

In which we offer a less than scientific discussion of the causes and symptoms of PMS, taking care to clearly avoid any reference to incomprehensible things such as prostaglandins, para-aminobenzoic acid, or tofu.

• • • • • • • • • • • •

Gwen's Story

No one believed me when I told them I might have PMS. My mother said I'd just inherited her whimsical Irish temperament; my father said I'd inherited my mother's bitchy Irish temperament. My boyfriend blamed my spaciness on nuclear fallout from the fifties. My sister, the dental hygienist, said my depression was from not flossing regularly. My best friend said my salt binges and breast tenderness had something to do with being thirty-four and not married. My doctor said I wasn't getting enough fiber in my diet. I finally went to another doctor. And she said that I definitely had PMS and that only one thing caused it: HORMONES.

Things That Do *Not* Cause PMS

Long-suspected but never technically proven, these cannot be blamed for bringing on premenstrual syndrome. Sorry.

▲ the greenhouse effect
▲ spandex
▲ cheap after-shave
▲ cellulite
▲ condoms
▲ the Dow-Jones average
▲ "Monday Night Football"
▲ cubic zirconias
▲ the price of the yen
▲ public transportation
▲ Communism
▲ microwave ovens
▲ bad perms
▲ summer reruns
▲ tight jeans
▲ radon

Things That Will *Not* Cure PMS

No matter what anybody says, none of the following will cure your PMS:

▲ pizza delivery boys
▲ crystals
▲ gene-splicing
▲ long-stemmed roses
▲ after-Christmas sales
▲ oat bran
▲ *glasnost*
▲ the *National Enquirer*
▲ channeling
▲ Donald Trump
▲ the ERA
▲ Godiva chocolate
▲ flying first class
▲ oral sex
▲ insider trading
▲ Tom Cruise
▲ cable TV
▲ losing your virginity
▲ a thousand points of light
▲ electrolysis
▲ Laura Ashley prints
▲ Retin-A

Welcome to the Wild and Wacky World of PMS

Maybe it wouldn't be so bad if we *only* craved chocolate, or we *only* got irritable, or we *only* went out and charged the VISA card to the max. But, unfortunately, PMS means premenstrual *syndrome*, and that means a mix of symptoms that don't always match. For example, it's hard to want to throw things when your eyes are so blurry, you can't see where you're aiming.

Let's just hope these symptom combinations don't happen to you:

headaches and increased sex drive	Known as getting him all hot and bewildered
excessive domesticity and clumsiness	Whatever you do, don't dust the knickknacks
sentimentality and extravagance	This is not the time to shop for Mother's Day
smell sensitivity and nausea	A hundred-foot distance from all Thai restaurants is recommended
food binging and lack of coordination	It's hard to stuff your face when you can't find it
ringing in ears and paranoia	No, it's *not* the IRS or that nerd from the health club at the door
compulsive spending and insomnia	Fortunately, the twenty-four-hour shopper probably can't get much of a wardrobe at 7-Eleven
nymphomania and poor judgment	The only thing worse than taking the consequences is getting a call from one of them

Easy Quiz #2
HOW TO TELL PMS FROM YOUR OWN STUPID CHARACTER FLAWS

Women often needlessly blame PMS instead of facing up to their own Stupid Character Flaws (SCF) or simply admitting that they might even just be Average, Normal Women (ANW).

Respond honestly to the problems below to help you answer the familiar question: "Is it me or is it PMS?"

1. Blurred vision
Occasionally, when you try to read the morning newspaper:
  a. the headlines all run together
  b. the headlines are in strange shapes and symbols
  c. the headlines depress you

Analysis
a: PMS. You are most likely experiencing premenstrual altered vision.
b: SCF. You have spent too much time watching television and the English language has become a series of meaningless characters, probably very much like your boyfriends.
c: ANW. You are a healthy American.

2. Excessive orderliness
Once a month, you stay late at the office to get organized:
  a. You tidy up your work area and go through your files.
  b. You tidy up your work area and go through your co-workers' files.
  c. It's midnight. You've vacuumed your office, Reception, and Personnel. Now you're repairing the copy machine.

Analysis
a: ANW. You're a conscientious worker.
b: SCF. You are a major snoop and nobody wants to carpool with you.
c: PMS. Check the calendar—and happy filing!

3. Increased sex drive
You are at a masquerade party when a very attractive William Shakespeare approaches and whispers a couple of couplets in your ear:

a. You respond with a sonnet that includes your phone number.

b. You tell him you'll ditch R2D2 so the two of you can make a little history of your own.

c. You fondle his codpiece and invite him and the cute Zorro in the corner to meet you down at the boathouse in five minutes.

Analysis
a: ANW. Hey, who wouldn't?
b: SCF. You are a tease and have probably fooled around with every droid in the galaxy.
c: PMS. Warning—your hormones are crashing the party. You'd be smart to avoid the Three Musketeers.

4. Irritability
You are driving down the street and *accidentally* run over the neighbor's attack dog:

a. You cry because the loss of any life diminishes you, even poor Beelzebub's.

b. You find it difficult to feel remorse, since now your children can walk to school without protective padding.

c. You back up and run over it again, just to make sure.

Analysis
a: SCF. Come on, it was a *pit bull*.
b: ANW. This is normal, and so are the flowers, cards, and envelopes of money you keep getting from the other neighbors.
c: PMS. No woman in her right mind would mess up those whitewalls for nothing.

5. Nail biting
You tend to keep your hands in your pockets or behind your back because:

a. you think they are unusually large

b. you are afraid of shaking hands with someone and contracting one of those disgusting diseases out there for which there is no cure

c. your monthly manicure usually involves biting off all your nails fifteen minutes after you ovulate

Analysis
a: ANW. Any large part is going to embarrass *someone*.
b: SCF. You should bring this up with your therapist next time. You *are* seeing one, right?
c: PMS. Better to bite them off than use them to force the supermarket manager to open up another checkout stand.

3
YOUR BODY,
YOURSELF,
YOUR PROBLEM

In which we encourage the reader to take control of her physical condition. A sobering chapter in which we reluctantly draw parallels between regular exercise, healthy diet, good habits, and relief from PMS symptoms.

• • • • • • • • • • • •

Dierdre's Story

Every article I read about PMS tells me I'm doing it all wrong: I'm not exercising, I'm not eating properly, I'm not taking the right vitamins, I'm not keeping track of my cycle. How can anyone with PMS do any of that when half the time I don't even have the energy to close my robe?

It's like I'm visiting in an alien body that doesn't understand the concept of normal human movement. It never fails. I wake up one morning and look in the mirror and a creature from the planet Urovary is staring back at me. Her misshapen body protrudes grotesquely from a nightgown I don't remember buying. She can't seem to get the toothpaste on the toothbrush and she stares uncomprehendingly into my makeup case. She puts on clothes two sizes too small, mixing gray tweeds with cotton pastels and white sandals. She pours boysenberry syrup over frozen egg rolls for breakfast and then deliberately smashes the plate before she leaves for work forty-five minutes late. This human impersonator only stays a few days and then she returns to her home planet. It's almost as though she were never here, except for the fact that for days afterward my neck keeps tilting strangely to the side. Is that part of PMS, too?

The Bent Neck-Huge Purse Theory

Like Dierdre, most of us can easily identify the most obvious PMS symptoms that torment us three to ten days every month. But there are always residual effects that we forget to associate with PMS: We spend three weeks trying to grow back the nails we chewed off in five minutes of premenstrual anxiety. We spend days looking for another butter dish to replace the one we drop-kicked into the den. And, like Dierdre, we wonder why our head tilts painfully to the side when necks have seemingly nothing to do with hormones.

FOUR PACKETS OF KLEENEX
(FOR SPONTANEOUS CRYING)

BIRTH CONTROL DEVICE
(FOR INCREASED SEX DRIVE)

VARIOUS MEDICATIONS:
EVENING-PRIMROSE OIL,
IRON SUPPLEMENT, **PMS**
MULTIVITAMIN

HEAVY PANCAKE MAKEUP
(FOR RAVAGED SKIN)

LAST MONTH'S GAS AND
LIGHT BILL YOU FORGOT TO MAIL

The answer may be found in the contents of Dierdre's purse. Everyone knows that like some feminine archaeological site, a woman's purse is a road map of contemporary society. But when the purse-carrier has PMS, the contents of her Hostage Handbag carry more than sociological significance; with all she needs just to make it through the day, the damned thing weighs a ton.

BELT REMOVED WHEN
YOU RETAINED SIX
POUNDS OF WATER AFTER LUNCH

FAMILY PHOTO TO
REMIND YOU WHAT
YOU'LL LOSE IF YOU JUMP

EXTRA SET OF HOUSE
KEYS FOR WHEN YOU
LOCK YOURSELF OUT

ROLEX WATCH YOU
THOUGHT WAS LOST

LOTTERY TICKET STUBS

HALF-EATEN CANDY BARS

CORDLESS
MINI-VAC TO
CLEAN AND
DUST WHEN-
EVER THE
MOOD STRIKES;
ALSO HELPFUL
FOR PICKING
UP BROKEN
GLASS, CHINA,
ETC.

BIBLE MARKED TO PSALMS
30:5: "WEEPING MAY
ENDURE FOR A NIGHT,
BUT JOY COMETH IN THE
MORNING"

ROLL OF QUARTERS TO
CALL LOCKSMITH

EYEDROPS AND SUN-
GLASSES FOR SENSITIVE,
BLURRY EYES

SCREWDRIVER FOR BREAK-
ING INTO THE HOUSE AF-
TER YOU'VE LOST YOUR
EXTRA SET OF KEYS

COCKTAIL NAPKIN WITH
REFERRAL TO A GOOD
PMS DOCTOR FROM THE
BARTENDER

WALKMAN AND RELAXA-
TION TAPE——YOU LEFT
THE HEADPHONES AT
HOME

The Hormone Hostage Cavalcade of Monthly Complaints: My Monthly Cycle-Minder

MY MONTHLY CYCLE-MINDER

Use this scale to rank the degree of each symptom:

🙂 okay, I can live with this

😖 touch me and I'll scream

😡 stop me before I kill

SYMPTOMS	DAY OF CYCLE													
	1	2	3	4	5	6	7	8	9	10	11	12	13	14
too tired to respirate	😖													
breasts block view of floor	😖	😖												
I can't taste any food because it doesn't spend enough time in my mouth														
English language fails to meet my requirements for self-expression													🙂	
I believe a mass murderer is hiding in my chimney														
an invisible sadist is giving me a lobotomy with a Black & Decker drill	😖	🙂											🙂	
my neighbor with the weed whacker has six minutes to live														
sex makes me nauseous														
nausea makes me sexy														
when I wear blue and white, someone drops a letter in my mouth	😖													
menstruation!	M	M	M		M	M								

Unless you are a really lazy sluggard who isn't interested in taking responsibility for her body, you will make yourself a Cycle-Minder chart like the one shown below. Along the left-hand side, write down your symptoms when they appear and mark the days of the month that they occur.

Keeping a monthly record of the frequency and degree of your PMS symptoms (e.g., anxiety, bloating, breast tenderness, etc.) will help you and your doctor evaluate your progress as well as give your kids something interesting to take to school for Show and Tell.

Here's an example of Janelle's chart for the month of December.

15	16	17	18	19	20	21	22	23	24	25	26	27	28	29	30	31

Field Guide
to the
Hormone Hostage

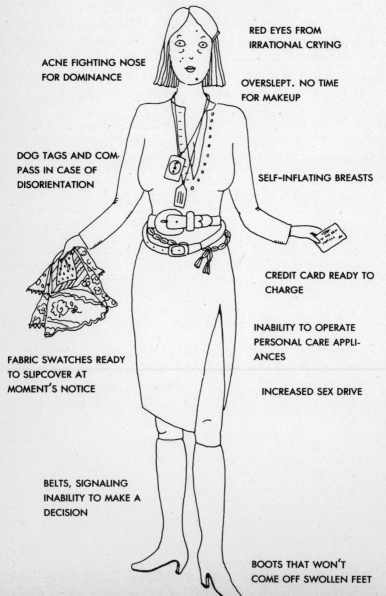

ACNE FIGHTING NOSE
FOR DOMINANCE

RED EYES FROM
IRRATIONAL CRYING

OVERSLEPT. NO TIME
FOR MAKEUP

DOG TAGS AND COM-
PASS IN CASE OF
DISORIENTATION

SELF-INFLATING BREASTS

CREDIT CARD READY TO
CHARGE

INABILITY TO OPERATE
PERSONAL CARE APPLI-
ANCES

FABRIC SWATCHES READY
TO SLIPCOVER AT
MOMENT'S NOTICE

INCREASED SEX DRIVE

BELTS, SIGNALING
INABILITY TO MAKE A
DECISION

BOOTS THAT WON'T
COME OFF SWOLLEN FEET

The Seven Warning Signs of the Questionable Medical Professional

You should never attempt any diet or exercise program without first consulting your doctor. Which brings up a good question: Who IS your doctor? How much do you really know about the one person who can get you out of your clothes without buying you dinner first? Is your gynecologist qualified to advise you in this specialized field?

Consult this handy and very scientific diagnostic tool to identify a less than ideal PMS management professional. In other words, when seeking a helpful gynecologist, AVOID ANY DOCTOR:

1. whose hobby is building little ships in bottles

2. who uses such phrases as "tinkle" and "your monthly friend"

3. whose office is easily identified by a neon sign outside

4. who subscribes only to *Money* magazine and *American Yachtsman*

5. who frequently stars in any of your fantasies involving leather or metal

6. who plays golf with your boss

7. who notes in your chart: "on the rag"

Aerobics and Death

(The No-Effort, Lose-a-Pound-a-Day, Shape, Trim, and Tone-Up Program for the Hormone Hostage Who Would Rather Die than Move)

This is the only exercise regimen you'll ever need and definitely the only one you're capable of.

Activity	Time	Target Area	Calories Expended
running the car back and forth over your wedding dress	1 hr.	hand/eye/foot coordination	30 (60 if you have a stick shift)
opening and closing the refrigerator door	3 min.	tones upper arm	50 (subtract from calories consumed while completing the exercise)
lying in the bathtub turning faucets on and off with your toes	3 hrs.	shapes ankles & calves	25
channel flipping to mindlessly watch everything on television	5 hrs.	strengthens eye muscles	2 (more if you have cable)
pulling control-top pantyhose over water-swollen thighs	1 hr.	tones lower back and shoulders	12 (28 if One Size Fits All)

Activity	Time	Target Area	Calories Expended
high-decibel screaming	2 days	improves breath control, circulation	80
changing clothes minimum of three times before work	35 min.	overall workout	50 (more if during winter months)
apologizing for your behavior	30 sec.	increases heart rate	100 (more if in court)
explaining to the doctor that you really DO need the Valium	20 min.	strengthens facial muscles	35 (more if it's your vet)
reapplication of blush to sallow skin	15 sec. (repeat 5 times a day)	tones wrist and neck	20

The Hormone Hostage Amazing Chocolate-and-Salt Diet

Every Hormone Hostage worth her progesterone knows the main ingredients of a healthy PMS management diet. But how can any woman be expected to choose intelligently between whole wheat bread and hot fudge brownie surprise when she's in an altered state of consciousness?

Below, here are the foods you probably should eat and the foods we know you WILL eat.

BREAKFAST

HEALTHY FOODS	"GET REAL" FOODS
cream of buckwheat cereal	Cocoa Puffs
honey	chocolate milk
nonfat milk	strawberry Pop-Tarts with
banana or pear	grape jelly
1 cup roasted grain beverage	6 cups of coffee with cream, Sweet 'N Low

MID-MORNING SNACK

HEALTHY FOODS	"GET REAL" FOODS
1 pecan bran muffin	box of assorted Danish
1 cup herb tea	4 cups coffee

LUNCH

HEALTHY FOODS	"GET REAL" FOODS
steamed vegetable platter	enchilada à la carte
applesauce	"garbage" burrito
10-grain roll, no butter	two bowls chips and salsa
iced herb tea with lemon	margarita grande
	flan

AFTERNOON SNACK

HEALTHY FOODS	"GET REAL" FOODS
1 small bag dried sunflower seeds mineral water	1 bag Doritos 3 Almond Joy bars Diet Coke

REALLY LATE AFTERNOON SNACK

HEALTHY FOODS	"GET REAL" FOODS
Granola bar	1 stale lemon-filled cruller

DINNER

HEALTHY FOODS	"GET REAL" FOODS
skinless chicken breast brown rice butternut squash marinated cucumber salad red raspberries 2 oatmeal cookies (sweetened with apple juice) sparkling water	buffalo wings with barbecue sauce & Roquefort dip 2 side orders pork rinds potato salad Black Forest torte à la mode carafe of the house rosé

EVENING SNACK

HEALTHY FOODS	"GET REAL" FOODS
1 handful carob-coated peanuts	1 bag chocolate semi-sweet morsels

NIGHTCAP

HEALTHY FOODS	"GET REAL" FOODS
camomile tea	amaretto and cream

MIDNIGHT SNACK

HEALTHY FOODS	"GET REAL" FOODS
1 rice cake 1 pineapple slice	2 orders sweet-and-sour pork 1 order dumplings double order almond cookies

Easy Quiz #3
WHAT'S YOUR PMS-IQ?

Match the following terms with their correct definitions.

1. Oil of Evening Primrose:
   a. a facial moisturizer you can buy at Woolworth's
   b. a Pulitzer Prize-winning play about incest in the South
   c. an essential fatty acid used to treat PMS symptoms

2. Progesterone:
   a. a hormone which, when overproduced in a woman's body, can create depression
   b. a pasta dish with three cheeses and squid
   c. the legendary site of a famous Western shoot-out in American folklore

3. Ovulate:
   a. a powdered hot or cold beverage favored by children in the fifties
   b. to applaud enthusiastically until a rock star has left the arena
   c. to release a fertile egg ten to fourteen days prior to menstruation

4. Hypothalamus:
   a. an extinct pachyderm distinguished by the extreme shortness of its appendages
   b. a gland which regulates menstruation
   c. a psychotic condition in which the patient believes he is one of the Marx Brothers

5. Dysmenorrhea:
   a. an ancient city located to the south of Tel Aviv
   b. menstrual cramps or discomfort
   c. the urge to pull the wings off butterflies

6. Estrogen:
   a. a Biblical heroine
   b. a character in *Waiting for Godot*
   c. a hormone which, if overproduced, can induce premenstrual anxiety

7. Mittelschmerz:
   a. "middle pain" occurring during ovulation
   b. a popular acrobatic dance troupe that employs ornate masks
   c. the original family name of Fred and Ethel Mertz

K E Y

If you can't figure these out on your own, put this book down, walk outside, and get
a life.

4

TAKING IT TO THE STREETS

In which we discuss practical methods of survival out there in a world where no one gives your hormones the time of day.

• • • • • • • • • • • • •

Lana's Story

The problem with my PMS is that no two months are ever alike. One month I can't wear synthetic fabrics without getting a rash. The next month, I can't wear cottons or silks. And the only bra that's ever comfortable is wool. Earrings turn my ears green and sometimes the sound of bacon sizzling gives me migraines. Every other month I spend an entire day in bed reading back issues of Ebony, and I'm not even black. I keep praying for the same two things: that someone will find a cure for PMS and that the one company in America that manufactures wool bras won't go out of business.

Days o' Death

As Lana will agree, some PMS days are much worse than others. For one or two days a month, or perhaps once every few months, a Hostage may undergo a metamorphosis so extreme that she will become virtually another person. This person is usually Attila the Hun or Joan Crawford. Occasionally certain similarities to Helen Keller will be noted. Whatever the resemblance, the transformation is so sudden and complete that the Hostage becomes traumatized and can be rendered incapable of functioning in the real world for a few hours or days.

It is during these Days o' Death that the Hostage is most likely to commit bizarre and totally uncharacteristic acts, such as chopping down the tree her parents planted when she was born or racing furtively through Sears and hiding Craftsman tools inside large appliances.

The Hormone Hostage must learn to recognize these days as temporary circumstances and begin to take positive steps toward minimizing their devastating effect on her daily life, not to mention her reputation.

PMS and the Decision-Making Process

Flexibility is the key to surviving premenstrual captivity. There are very few things that absolutely cannot wait until you get your period. Life-changing decisions should not be arrived at when you're having trouble putting on your pantyhose and you can't remember whom you just talked to on the phone. Remember Scarlett O'Hara. Think about it tomorrow. After all, tomorrow is another day and your estrogen level could go up by then.

▲ *Decisions Not to Make While Held Hostage*

- ▲ wallpaper patterns

- ▲ permanent eyeliner

- ▲ term or whole life insurance

- ▲ size, shape, and placement of a tattoo

- ▲ breast reduction

- ▲ the wording on your vanity license plate

- ▲ the future of your invalid parents

- ▲ tubal ligation

- ▲ pre-need funeral arrangements

Good Reading Material When You're Trying Not to Eat, Cry, or Maim Something

▲ *Leaves of Gold*

▲ *Gifts from the Sea*

▲ *Country Quilts and Crafts* magazine (avoid Christmas issues)

▲ The Sierra Club Calendar

▲ *The Little Prince*

▲ *Fascinating Womanhood*

▲ *The Whole Earth Catalog*

▲ *Sonnets from the Portuguese*

▲ *Think and Grow Rich*

▲ *All Creatures Great and Small*

▲ *I Hate to Cook Book*

▲ Burpee's seed catalog

▲ *Arizona Highways* magazine

Do Not Read These Things

Hostages beware:

▲ *Soldier of Fortune* magazine

▲ anything by Elisabeth Kübler-Ross

▲ *The Bell Jar*

▲ *In Search of Excellence*

▲ *The Second Sex*

▲ *The Tiffany Wedding*

▲ *My Mother, Myself*

▲ *Fit for Life*

▲ *The Velveteen Rabbit*

▲ Joe Weider's *Shape* magazine

▲ back issues of *Gourmet*

▲ *The Handmaid's Tale*

Your Bed, Your Best Friend

As every Hormone Hostage can testify, there are days in the life of a woman when it is best not to venture beyond your dust ruffle. Your life and the lives of those you love may depend upon your ability to withdraw from polite society and confine yourself to matters that can only be accomplished from a prone position. Here are a few:

▲ do a breast self-examination

▲ pumice your callouses

▲ dial 976 numbers at random

▲ bone up on the community property laws in your state

▲ play darts

▲ using a flashlight and mirror, explore the inner recesses of your body

▲ check the expiration dates of everything in your nightstand

▲ choose a new ceiling color

▲ tear off the "penalty of law" tags from your pillows

▲ dismantle your snooze alarm

▲ see if you can rotate your mattress without getting out of bed

▲ teach yourself card tricks

▲ moisturize

▲ begin composing this year's Christmas letter

▲ deface the pictures of models in old *Glamour* magazines

Twenty Things the Hormone Hostage Should Avoid Completely

▲ your mother

▲ shopping for swimsuits

▲ wine tastings

▲ karate class

▲ confession

▲ buffets

▲ 'The Twilight Zone" marathons

▲ the Spiegel catalog

▲ automated teller machines

▲ shortcuts to the freeway

▲ the Department of Motor Vehicles

▲ doing your own nails

▲ construction sites

▲ Outward Bound

▲ team sports

▲ home improvement expos

▲ the state of Nevada

▲ Cuisinarts and potato peelers

▲ subtitled foreign films

▲ henna

Celluloid Hell

When PMS strikes, these movies get a Two-Thumbs-Down:

▲ *Fatal Attraction*

▲ *Mommie Dearest*

▲ *The Three Faces of Eve*

▲ *Carrie*

▲ *Sophie's Choice*

▲ *The Stepford Wives*

▲ *Dark Victory*

▲ *Red Sonja*

▲ anything with Mamie Van Doren

▲ *Carnal Knowledge*

▲ *Yentl*

▲ *Interiors*

▲ *Nine to Five*

▲ *Pink Flamingos*

▲ *Diary of a Mad Housewife*

▲ *Mars Needs Women*

▲ *The Graduate*

▲ *Ilsa, She-Bitch of the SS*

▲ *Move Over, Darling*

▲ *When Women Had Tails*

▲ anything with the word "Porky" or "Conqueror" in the title

Seize the Day Before It Seizes You

Knowledge is power and power doesn't do you any good if you're having trouble forming complete sentences. But powerful is the Hormone Hostage who knows enough to anticipate her worst days. She will make plans in advance to ensure that her life goes on, even if she can't.

▲ What Can You Do Ahead of Time?

lose six pounds

coordinate your clothes and jewelry; accessorize enough for five days

prepare a week's worth of Seal-A-Meals

make copies of your birth certificate, driver's license, etc., and tape them to your body

trace often-traveled routes on a local street map and affix to dashboard

trim down your nails

make peace with your God

balance your checkbook

program your VCR

Easy Quiz #4

SHOULD YOU REMAIN PRONE?

(A Basic Barometer to Determine if Getting Out of Bed Will Be Hazardous to Your Health)

▲ *Circle the answer that most applies to you.*

1. **I awaken with a feeling of:**
   a. fatigue
   b. doom
   c. conviction that if I rolled over and died, no one would miss me until my rent was due

2. **The only thing that could get me out of bed today is:**
   a. the pizza delivery boy
   b. a fire
   c. the remote control being broken

3. **If I go to work, I know I will:**
   a. close my door and take a nap
   b. nod off in the middle of a meeting
   c. sleep through closing time and get locked in the building overnight

4. **From where I lie:**
   a. the wallpaper is moving
   b. ceiling cracks are widening
   c. I'm in the corner having an out-of-body experience

5. **The smell of coffee brewing in the kitchen:**
   a. is nauseating
   b. actually smells more like hot radiator fluid and cologne from Woolworth's
   c. disturbs me because no one else is home

K E Y

If your answers included more a's than b's or c's, go to work, try to look busy, then go home early and go back to bed.

If your answers were mostly b's, call in with a good excuse, such as you're feeling fluish and you don't want to spread any germs.

If your answers were heavy on the c's, the fact that you are still employed anywhere is a good thought to meditate on as you lie motionless for the next twenty-four hours.

5

THE HOLISTIC HORMONE HOSTAGE

In which we offer an enlightened approach to self-healing when our karmas are in limbo and our auras are in "Park." Includes words of encouragement excerpted from actual poems, journals, and other creative expressions from the troubled pens of Hormone Hostages who live in real cities and towns just like yours. A source of inspiration for women who are into that sort of stuff.

• • • • • • • • • • • • •

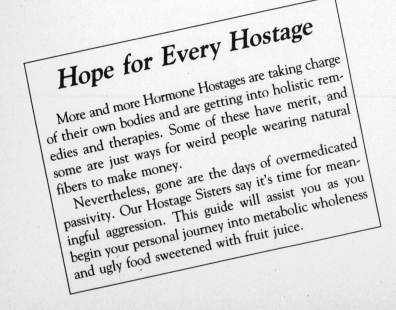

Hope for Every Hostage

More and more Hormone Hostages are taking charge of their own bodies and are getting into holistic remedies and therapies. Some of these have merit, and some are just ways for weird people wearing natural fibers to make money.

Nevertheless, gone are the days of overmedicated passivity. Our Hostage Sisters say it's time for meaningful aggression. This guide will assist you as you begin your personal journey into metabolic wholeness and ugly food sweetened with fruit juice.

Rachel's Story

Once a month, I used to stand in the Xerox room at work and cry for all the dead trees. If I'd had caffeine or a doughnut that day, it would be worse. Just the sight of redwood patio furniture could throw me into mourning for the earth and her wooden fruit. Since I never considered myself the sensitive type, I decided that I had PMS.

My girlfriend Bunny suggested that I try herbal teas and yoga exercises. I just wanted a pill to take it all away. She said I should listen to flute music and write letters to my hormones. I just wanted to sleep. She said I should make friends with my PMS. I just wanted to kill it.

Finally, Bunny reminded me of the times she used to throw dirt clots into the neighbors' pool once a month until she learned to handle her PMS naturally. It was then I realized that I could let PMS rule my emotions, or I could turn it into something meaningful. I became a Holistic Hostage and now my life has changed. I still cry in the Xerox room, but now it's a natural and beautiful experience.

Alternative Therapies

If all you've done to attack your PMS is ask your doctor to prescribe something to knock you out for three days, you haven't fully explored your options. The following treatments have offered varying degrees of relief to some and amusement to others. (Check your local Yellow Pages—these are not available or legal in some states, such as those east of California.)

acupressure   As if all your buttons weren't being pressed already.

acupuncture   Don't try "Dr. Ho's Home Version" on video.

aroma therapy   Loosely based on the concept that if you keep your nose busy, you won't care what's going on with the rest of you.

aversion therapy   Imagine snapping yourself with a rubber band every time you feel paranoid.

biofeedback   Think long and hard before attaching yourself to electrical appliances. Gives you more information about yourself than anyone really wants.

bloodletting   Archaic, not to mention difficult to find a licensed practitioner.

chiropractic   Only if you can stand the sound of it.

colonics   The concept seems to miss the point as far as we're concerned.

foot reflexology   Soak your feet, walk on marbles, and save fifty dollars.

herbology   Has its advantages, but find out what they used for fertilizer.

hydrotherapy   Right. As if you need more water.

hypnosis	Ask for the Post-Hypnotic Suggestion Special: Every time you hear the refrigerator door open, you hit the floor and do ten sit-ups.
leeching	See "bloodletting."
meditation	The idea is to get your mind *off* your problems.
nutritional therapy	So easy to do and so inexpensive, nobody wants to try it.
primal therapy	Chances are you've been screaming yourself senseless for years and didn't know what to call it. Why dredge up that unhappy childhood when you're ovulating?
rebirthing	Unless you can rebirth yourself as an heiress, don't bother.
self-gratification	Pretty much says it all.
visualization	Picture yourself in a safe, beautiful world where there are no hormones.
yoga	If you can stand the pain of yoga, PMS should be a breeze.

Self-Expression

Historically, the Hormone Hostage has always found relief in self-expression. In the past, these expressions have been limited mostly to the destruction of breakable objects such as glass, china, and new relationships with innocent men.

Recently, however, many Hostages have found it helpful to redirect their energies into more creative avenues. In the following pages we offer examples of journals, poetry, and other artistic expression from the minds and hearts of actual Hostages. These not only serve as effective stress-reducing techniques but are also valuable examples of why you should never put anything important on paper.

Hostage Haiku

Melodic sparrow on my sill
What do you think as you lay your egg?
Too late. I've shot you.

> *Fumiko O.*
> *3200 B.C.*

The way to my lover's house is long
I wish I could remember
Where the hell he lives

> *Hattie G.*
> *1845*

Tinkling glass on tile
"I didn't do it, Mommy!"
Death, come quickly

> *Eleanor B.*
> *1989*

Ode to Mrs. Fields

There you are
waiting for me
In the mall
Was it just last month
we were here?
Me, with my sixteen shopping bags
You, with those expensive red tins
brimming with fresh-baked satisfaction.
I tried to walk by
But you whispered aromatically in my ear
"Sister!
Let me love you
Let me fill you
As only women can love each other
Wholly
Completely
With Oatmeal Raisin
And Macadamia Nuts
And chunks
And chunks
Of chocolate."
Debbie,
You are Forever
In my heart
On my lips
And on my thighs
I'll see you again
Next month

Mary B.
1988

A Song to Jason
(Part One)

(Written by Jan S. Three Days Before Her Period. 6:30 P.M.)

The kids are at mom's
The glasses are chilling
Soft music is playing
And I'm oh so willing

Jason, Tommy's soccer coach, is coming to dinner!

The doorbell rings
And I dim the light
One more spritz of perfume
Oh, glorious night!

Jason, who wants me, is coming to dinner!

[NOTE: In the intervening hours between Jan's first giddy poem with its joyous, childlike rhythms and her second, more somber elegy, a significant transformation has occurred. From her earlier fantasy world she has crashed through reality and spiraled even farther downward to unrealistic depths of self-loathing. This is a typical PMS mood swing, most likely aggravated by that sugary dessert glop she baked just for Jason.]

(Part Two)

(10:30 P.M.)

Oh, Grave!
I would come to thee freely
Were it not that
Tommy has practice in the morning at nine.

Oh, Humiliation!
You mock me in your rugby shirt
and scorn me
with your youthful
Indifference.

Oh, Love,
Why must you visit
Only to forego the expensive
tiger shrimp
and ask for a burger?

Oh, Life.
I must press on.
I must face you again
Tomorrow.
But this time Tommy can walk
To practice.

Jan S.
1990

▲ *One Woman's Road*

Kathy's Journal Entries

(The following are complete and unedited journal entries of Kathy T., a thirty-three-year-old Hormone Hostage. These excerpts describe the horrendous days in March of 1986 before she was accurately diagnosed. Note the overall tone of hopelessness and general incoherence.)

DAY 1—THE FIRST DAY OF MY PERIOD—
The doctor says I should write in my journal every day. I hate him. He says writing everything down and reviewing it with him every month will help him understand what's going on. All *I* understand is that this is costing me a fortune.

DAY 8—
Feeling fine. I must have just been having a particularly bad month. Probably due to the combination of smog and new sexual positions. Bob seems to need variety, but I worry about his asthma. I probably don't need to go back to the doctor. How old is that nurse of his anyway? I bet she hasn't menstruated three months in a row yet. And why does she always have to stay in the room?

DAY 12—
Had a weird dream about Dr. Oliver's nurse. Bob was wheezing and she kept pounding him on the back but he seemed to like it. I was trying to help him, but I was sitting in a tub full of butterscotch sauce and I didn't want to get the bathroom floor dirty.

DAY 14—
I know I'm ovulating because all I want to do is make love
and bite the heads off gummy bears. I'm so disoriented,
I'm afraid to drive to the doctor's today. But if I miss my
appointment, they'll still charge me. I hate that nurse.
I bet she reads my files aloud to her friends at Happy Hour.

DAY 18—
I'm feeling really depressed. I snapped at the doorman
this morning for being so damned jovial. Then I started
crying. I knew the doctor would want to see me like this,
so I took time off to go in. It was my third lunch hour today.

DAY 20—
I called up Bob for no reason and told him I wanted to break
it off. He told me to wait ten days and we'd discuss it then.
He seemed a little curt. I wonder if he's seeing someone
else? What does he see in me, anyway?

DAY 23—
Another strange dream last night. I was walking through
Woodstock. Somebody told me a baby was being born under
the Pepsi Challenge tent. I walked over and held the infant
in my arms. She was only seconds old, but I recognized her.
Dr. Oliver's nurse.

DAY 26—
Bob is . . . I mean, I just can't . . . I honestly . . .
Food is the only thing I . . . I hate that nurse . . . I
am so huge . . . People look at me weird . . . Damn, why
can't I just . . . I am NOT going to Sally's wedding in
August . . .

DAY 27—

DAY 28—
Doctor's exam room. Nurse Twit comes in. Tells me to ''hop
up on the table.'' I reach for the speculum on her tray and
hold it to her throat. She keeps screaming, ''I don't know
Bob. I don't know anyone named Bob.'' Doctor comes in.
Tells me to hop up on the table. Says maybe I do have a little
PMS. Says he wants to refer me to someone else. In the mean-
time, I'm supposed to keep writing in my journal.

DAY 2—NEW CYCLE—
I got my period yesterday. A few cramps, but I feel great.
Bob asked me if I still wanted to break up. Who knows what
he's talking about. I think he asks me that every month or
so because he's feeling insecure. That cute nurse at Dr.
Oliver's called and reminded me I'm supposed to see a spe-
cialist next week about my hormones. But I probably won't
go. I really feel fine. I love her hair. I've got to ask her
where she gets it cut . . .

Easy Quiz #5

"I OVULATE, THEREFORE I AM"

There's no guessing on this quiz! The answers are not supplied; they must come from you, the real you, the holistic you. There are no right answers, only honest ones. Feel free to write on this page and use more paper if you need it. Or write on the walls or parts of your body. Anything that seems really spontaneous and self-indulgent.

1. If your womb was an animal, what would it be?

2. Imagine yourself sitting across the table from your pituitary gland. What questions would you like to ask?

3. Draw a peaceful, pastoral scene. Now place yourself in the setting. Now draw your ovaries in the setting. (What time of year is it? Are there any cows in the picture? Did you use more than one color?)

6
THE HORMONE HOSTAGE IN SOCIETY

In which we offer a historical perspective of premenstrual syndrome through the ages as viewed through literature, culture, superstition, popular thought, and lots of unpopular scuttlebutt.

• • • • • • • • • • • • •

Patience's Story

(The following is an excerpt from a letter written by a young woman in England to her friend in the New World almost four hundred years ago. This invaluable historical artifact documents what we can now recognize as an acute case of PMS.)

(The letter is on display in its entirety in the PMS Wing of the Women's Museum of Contemporary Maladies in Fargo, North Dakota.)

Plymouth, England
February 22, 1622

Dearest Prudence,

It has been nigh unto two years since thou didst take your leave on the Mayflower, yet only today have I received thy first dispatch from the New World. The mails be slow. . . .

. . . How wonderful that your journey brought you to a place called New Plymouth. Some coincidence, huh?

Would that I had not missed the boat. I was nearly packed and was only desirous of choosing which frock to wear for the trip, but I couldn't decide between the brown one and the brown one. By the time I chose the brown one, it mattered not, as I retained the waters, (as I am wont to do).

I lay me down but for moment to calm the pains in my head and would have slept through the night but for those annoying vesper bells. I tooketh up my bag and sprinteth toward the docks in hopes of still joining you and your kin, but I boarded the wrong vessel and spent the Spring trying to find a Huguenot who would give me passage home. . . .

. . . Your report of a Thanksgiving feast calls to mind the very dinner I ate last night. Pies, fowl, fish, pies, puddings, ale, pies, and a multitude of after-dinner mints. Of course, there were no Indians or anyone else, for that matter, with whom to share my supper. Which was just fine with me. . . .

. . . I keep you ever in my prayers and thoughts, and oft are the times I smile and recall how we dreamt together of the New World. And now you're there and I'm still here. But I've got chocolate.

Your devoted friend,
Patience

Patience

Landmarks in PMS History

ca. 4000 B.C.

The 30-day Egyptian calendar is devised. Dawn of the Monthly Cycle.

ca. 3000 B.C.

Sumerians introduce beer. Alcohol intolerance becomes symptom of PMS.

ca. 2700 B.C.

Metal mirrors invented.

ca. 2699 B.C.

Acne cover-stick invented.

ca. 1500 B.C.

Percussion instruments used in music. First recorded murder of a drummer by a premenstrual lute player.

ca. 950 B.C.

Israel designs first caftan. Water-retaining women flood marketplace.

ca. 200 B.C.

Price in Rome for female slaves: $1,000. Premenstrual slaves marked down to $12.95.

30 B.C.

Cleopatra chooses death over life without Marc Antony and those Baci balls he always brought from Rome.

16 A.D.

Diamonds first mentioned; women begin to leave them on the sink.

31 A.D.

First recorded case of premenstrual domesticity: An obsessed Martha dusts while Mary entertains Jesus Christ in the living room.

ca. 620 A.D.

China begins production of porcelain. Hormone Hostages have something satisfying to break.

800 A.D.

Roses are cultivated in Europe; Hostage Husbands find new way to apologize for things they didn't do.

885 A.D.

The Book of the Roads and Countries published; disoriented Hostages find their way home.

942 A.D.

Linen produced; Hostages forget to turn iron off.

996 A.D.

Cane sugar introduced to Venice; female gondoliers lost at sea.

1118 A.D.

Doomed love affair with Abelard sends Héloïse into nunnery; first mention of concurrent cycles among roommates.

1202 A.D.

Court jesters first used to cheer up royal pains.

1428 A.D.

Joan of Arc hears voices.

1500 A.D.

Husbands of
Lucretia Borgia
start dropping
like flies.

1503 A.D.

Leonardo da Vinci
paints "Mona
Lisa"; adds smile.

1516 A.D.

Coffee introduced
to Europe; women
now stay awake
to enjoy PMS.

1520 A.D.

Chocolate
introduced to
Europe; women
have something to
crave besides
caffeine.

1533 A.D.

First lunatic
asylums filled with
women who had
too much coffee
and chocolate.

1594 A.D.

Shakespeare
writes *The Taming
of the Shrew*.

1612 A.D.

Manhattan
becomes a
trading center;
colonial Hostages
await January
white sales.

1688 A.D.

Plate glass developed;
women have something
to aim china at.

1692 A.D.

Salem finds
burning at stake
an extreme but
effective cure for
PMS.

1738 A.D.

First cuckoo clocks;
women become violent
on the hour.

1777 A.D.

Betsy Ross uses
her nesting
instincts to serve
her country.

1789 A.D.

Marie Antoinette
goes on sugar
binge; French
people
unsympathetic.

1801 A.D.

Chocolate maker
John Cadbury
born.

1814 A.D.

Dolly Madison runs
back into burning
White House to save
portrait of George
Washington and a
three-pound box of
French bonbons.

Francis Scott Key writes
national anthem; only
women with severe PMS
can sing the high notes.

1836 A.D.

Samuel Colt patents
pistol; children learn
to finish their
vegetables.

1850 A.D.

Elizabeth Barrett
Browning asks
"How do I love
thee?" and loses
count.

1853 A.D.

Bloated wife of
E.G. Otis inspires
installation of first
elevator.

1860 A.D.

A hormonally-
crazed Queen
Victoria terrorizes
the palace; Prince
Albert hides in a
can.

1866 A.D.

Alfred Nobel
invents dynamite;
children don't
even have to be
told to eat their
vegetables.

1871 A.D.

Great Chicago
Fire—Mrs.
O'Leary leaves
iron on; blames
cow.

1889 A.D.

John Cadbury
dies.

1898 A.D.

Sigmund Freud
keeps asking:
"What does a
woman want?"
Women reply:
"Eat Id and die."

1907 A.D.

French model has
bad PMS; Picasso
discovers cubism.

1920 A.D.

Easy credit just
gets easier and
easier.

1923 A.D.

Sanka is invented.

1926 A.D.

Gertrude Ederle
gets fed up with
the kids; swims
English Channel
to get fourteen
hours of solitude.

1927 A.D.

Lizzie Borden's
parents deny
existence of PMS.

1929 A.D.

Great Stock
Market Crash;
men get an idea
of what women
go through every
month.

1930 A.D.

Twinkies, Snickers
bars, and
Plexiglas change
the face of PMS.

1931 A.D.

Gambling and
six-month divorces
are legalized in
Nevada. Las
Vegas Hostage
population rises.

"The Hormonal
Causes of
Premenstrual
Tension" carves
Dr. Robert Frank
a niche in
Hostage History.

1933 A.D.

Prohibition repealed.

1939 A.D.

Gone with the Wind proves that mint juleps and PMS don't mix.

1942 A.D.

Wartime sugar-rationing gives Hostages some emotional relief until Disney releases *Bambi*.

1944 A.D.

Banner year for Hostage music lovers with hit songs "I Should Care," "Ac-cent-tchu-ate the Positive," "Don't Fence Me In," and "I'll Walk Alone."

1947 A.D.

Bikini makes a splash.

1950 A.D.

Dr. Katharina Dalton injects herself daily with progesterone; cures her PMS migraines but can no longer wear short sleeves.

1952 A.D.

George Jorgensen becomes Christine with the understanding that she can never use PMS as an excuse for anything.

1956 A.D.

Lerner and Loewe ask the musical question "Why can't a woman be more like a man?" Eliza Doolittle answers, "Kiss my ascot."

1963 A.D.

Hormones plus zero gravity bring down Russian astronaut Valentina Tereshkova.

1966 A.D.

Dr. Timothy Leary declares "Turn On, Tune In, Drop Out." Hostages realize they don't need drugs to do that.

1967 A.D.

Twiggy takes all the fun out of premenstrual binging.

1970 A.D.

Anniversary of women's suffrage. Hostages celebrate fifty years of misplacing their sample ballot.

1976 A.D.

Edgy Hostages go underground as loud noises and explosive fireworks mark the two hundredth birthday of the United States.

1982 A.D.

Designer chocolates, designer sheets, designer water, designer cookies, etc., give Yuppie Hormone Hostages a new perspective on PMS.

1986 A.D.

Over-the-counter PMS medications replace Lite beer as the remedy of choice.

1990 A.D.

Raging Hormones coins the phrase "Hormone Hostage." Women learn to laugh and ovulate simultaneously.

Should a Woman Be President?

Society has often given hormones as the reason why women should not hold our nation's highest office. We've all heard the scenario in which a female President would, with one premenstrual outburst, impulsively push The Button and begin World War III.

We say the question is not *should* a woman be President, but, why would any woman want to be President? Any qualified person, male or female, should be able to occupy the Oval Office. But so far, only men have been naive enough to look forward to it.

Here are a few reasons why most women don't even WANT to be President:

▲ Everybody criticizes your clothes.

▲ Everyone will find out that you avoided fulfilling your college PE requirements twenty years ago.

▲ Mike Wallace will keep track of your menstrual cycle.

▲ You have to go to the funerals of people you didn't even know.

▲ When you visit a foreign country, you can't bargain down the vendors.

▲ You have to use a gynecologist from The Walter Reed Army Medical Center.

▲ If you break out, Dan Rather talks about it.

▲ Your children will grow up and write whole books about three bad days you had when they were in fifth grade.

▲ You'll have to eat everything they serve you when countries have you over for dinner.

▲ Men in dark suits with earphones will follow you into the bathroom.

▲ All those people from Iowa will want to come and tour your house every summer.

▲ *People* magazine will pay big bucks for a picture of you in your swimsuit.

Little-Known Facts About PMS

▲ All sightings of Elvis Presley in the last ten years have been reported by women whose PMS levels exceeded the national norm.

▲ Sixty-five percent of control-top panty hose are purchased by women three days before their period.

▲ *I Hate My Life*, the first musical about PMS, was produced in Boston in 1971, but closed after one performance due to scathing reviews that called the piece "another work of fiction by women."

▲ Average time a postmenstrual woman will take to select dinner from a restaurant menu: 3 minutes.

▲ Average time a premenstrual woman will take to select dinner from a restaurant menu: 16 minutes.

▲ Amount of hot rolls consumed while deciding: 4.5.

▲ Longest time a Hormone Hostage has spent in her room, in bed, alone, with the door locked: 16.5 days. Janice Zick of Framingham, Massachusetts, spent over two weeks in her upstairs bedroom arbitrarily ordering unisex clothing from L.L. Bean, J. Crew, and Lands' End. She only emerged to sign the UPS receipts.

▲ Percentage of Hormone Hostages who own Barry Manilow albums: 77.

▲ Between the years of 1930 and 1958, forty-five hormone hostages took over an abandoned convent and formed the short-lived cult known as the "little sisters of Joan Crawford." These obscure novitiates devoted themselves to inflicting perpetual suffering and keeping their habits on wooden hangers.

▲ Number of accordion players who received death threats from Hormone Hostages in 1983: 218.

▲ Percentage of American twelve-year-olds who cannot locate the United States on a map of the world: 22.

▲ Percentage of Hormone Hostages who cannot locate a map of the world: 49.

▲ Percentage of Hormone Hostages who have converted to the metric system: 0.

▲ Average lifespan of a parrot owned by a Hormone Hostage: 14 days.

Easy Quiz #6

HOSTAGE ON A HOT TIN ROOF

Tennessee Williams had a knack for finding the PMS in all of us. But the great premenstrual literary characters surely have not been limited to neurotic Southern belles. Throughout history, PMS has made a unique contribution to great literature as the inspiration of numerous books and plays.

Match the famous literary heroine with her infamous PMS symptom.

1. Blanche DuBois/A *Streetcar Named Desire*

2. Fanny Hill

3. Alice in Wonderland

4. Anna Karénina

5. Laura/*The Glass Menagerie*

6. Daisy/*The Great Gatsby*

7. Hester Prynne/*The Scarlet Letter*

8. Miss Havisham/*Great Expectations*

9. Mrs. de Winter/*Rebecca*

10. Nora/*A Doll's House*

a. poor judgment

b. excessive domesticity

c. increased sex drive

d. gross sentimentalism

e. disorientation

f. paranoia

g. withdrawal

h. delusions of grandeur

i. extravagance

j. suicidal urges

K E Y

1. (h) 2. (c) 3. (e) 4. (j) 5. (g) 6. (i) 7. (a) 8. (d) 9. (f) 10. (b)

If you actually read the above works, add five points to your score. If you only saw the movies, deduct five points from your score. If you rented the movies and watched them in bed while you ate peanut butter cups and Cheez-Its, you are practically a tragic heroine yourself—add ten points to your score.

7
PMS Is
Everybody's
Business

In which we explore the pitfalls of taking your hormones to work and conclude that most Hormone Hostages may be wise to marry money and remove themselves from the work force completely.

• • • • • • • • • • • • •

Jackie's Story

I used to get so annoyed with Cheryl, the whiny receptionist in Research that all the guys thought was so cute. One pre-menstrual pimple or ounce of excess water weight and she was home with her feet up, calling in sick. Or else, all you had to do was look at her sideways and she was in the bathroom crying. Honestly! I have PMS ten times worse than that zero and I'm in management! Believe you me, the company couldn't last a day without this little soldier, pre-, post-, or mid-menstrual. Why, there have been entire weeks when I was in the wrong office on the wrong floor punching the wrong buttons, but nothing kept me from tracking those satellites.

The Hormone Hostage on the Job

Jackie's insistence that PMS does not interfere with her daily performance is an example of self-delusion, a not uncommon symptom that probably creates problems for her with her co-workers and possibly jeopardizes her career, not to mention the safety of the free world. On the other hand, the self-indulgence of Cheryl, the receptionist, typifies many who are probably just pulling a paycheck until they get one of the guys in Research to marry them. Women like this hold us all up to ridicule and should be flogged.

Do's and Don'ts in the Premenstrual Workplace

DON'T:

▲ attempt to negotiate a raise or promotion

▲ flirt with the CEO in the elevator

▲ use the elevator (take the stairs)

▲ take business trips that require connecting flights

▲ write performance evaluations

▲ ask for a performance evaluation

▲ return calls from irate clients

▲ sign a United Way pledge card

▲ drink at lunch

▲ open the classifieds

▲ have your picture taken for a new photo badge

▲ enroll in the leadership training seminar

▲ confide to a coworker that you had an abortion in '71

DO:

▲ delegate

▲ bring doughnuts for everyone at the office

▲ keep six for yourself

▲ use accumulated sick days

▲ sign up for the corporate wellness program

▲ calculate your year-end bonus

▲ avoid freeway traffic and take the van pool

▲ plan your vacation

▲ hold all calls

▲ When all else fails, give blood. It lets you lie down and eat cookies at the same time.

Jobs Just for You

Tailor-made careers for the Hormone Hostage:

▲ princess

▲ vintner

▲ quality control inspector

▲ warden

▲ jackhammer operator

▲ museum docent

▲ nun

▲ postal clerk

▲ food critic

▲ divorce attorney

▲ meter maid

▲ mime

▲ butcher

Hormone Hostages Need Not Apply

The Hormone Hostage should seriously consider the ramifications of these career choices:

▲ children's barber

▲ flight navigator

▲ soft gelatin encapsulator

▲ crisis intervention counselor

▲ bakery counter clerk

▲ labor negotiator

▲ pharmacist

▲ electrologist

▲ cruise director

▲ camp counselor

▲ model

▲ pearl restringer

▲ police dispatcher

Easy Quiz #7

THE WILLIAMSON-SHEETS PERSONALITY PROFILE TO DETERMINE EMPLOYMENT SUITABILITY

For each statement, circle the answer which is the *most* correct. Do not take time to contemplate your response. Give your first reaction.

Remember, there are no right or wrong answers.

1. I seem to make friends:
  a. easily
  b. with difficulty
  c. only after a few drinks
  d. postmenstrually

2. Among my coworkers, I am considered to be:
  a. a respected leader
  b. a valued team member
  c. a clock-watching suit
  d. a ticking bomb

3. If I knew I could get away with it, I would:
  a. take home office supplies
  b. extend my lunch hour
  c. pad my expense account
  d. file for PMS disability

4. I consider my work to be:
  a. more important than my personal life
  b. as important as my personal life
  c. I have no personal life
  d. I have no life

5. I am willing to work weekends:
  a. never
  b. occasionally
  c. only under special circumstances
  d. as long as I'm not ovulating

6. I believe someone is monitoring my phone calls:
  a. not at all
  b. possibly
  c. not likely
  d. only when my breasts are tender

7. To me, the most important factor in my vocation is:
  a. personal fulfillment
  b. flexible hours
  c. understanding boss
  d. liberal sick day policy

8. I left my last position because:
  a. I disagreed with the management philosophy
  b. I wanted to pursue other career options
  c. I wanted to increase my income
  d. I forgot where they put the office

K E Y

There is no key to Easy Quiz #7, as results of this test are confidential and evaluated objectively on an individual basis. In other words, would *you* hire you?

8

A Hormone Is a Terrible Thing to Waste

In which we discuss the mind of the Hormone Hostage and its many mysteries, such as why a woman can run into a department store for a long-line bra and walk out with a six-pack of Duracells and a new dinette.

• • • • • • • • • • • • •

Debbie's Story

(In the following transcript of Debbie's interview, note her classic symptoms of PMS Panic: her sense of urgency in unimportant matters, her inability to focus on the subject at hand, her incompatibility with the space-time continuum, and an obsessive fixation on vegetables.)

I don't see what this PMS fuss is all about. My period is three days away, and I am just fine. I don't have headaches. I don't bloat. I don't break out, or cry, or lose my temper. I'm fine. I'm always fine. Nothing bothers me.

Except maybe that last earthquake in California. I know, I live in Chicago. But you can't be too careful. That's why I bought six hundred dollars worth of flash-lights and canned hash last month. I only meant to get a first aid kit for the car, but the more I thought about it, the more obvious it was that I'd darned well better be ready if The Big One ever came to Illinois.

I suppose you think that's funny. Well, sometimes, something just tells me ''Debbie, *do this now*.'' And it always seems right at the moment. Like yesterday, when I needed to pull off the freeway and have flames painted on the hood of my car. For me, then, it was the right thing to do.

Do you like this dress? I don't know. It's not my best color. I used to think it was, but now I look in the mirror and it makes me look like a turnip. I know, who's ever seen an electric blue turnip? But that's how I feel. I should really change out of this. I really should. You know, everything in my closet makes me look turnipy. Is there a mall somewhere around here?

(end of transcript)

Debbie Does the Mall

In search of a replacement top for her blender, Debbie enters the mall.

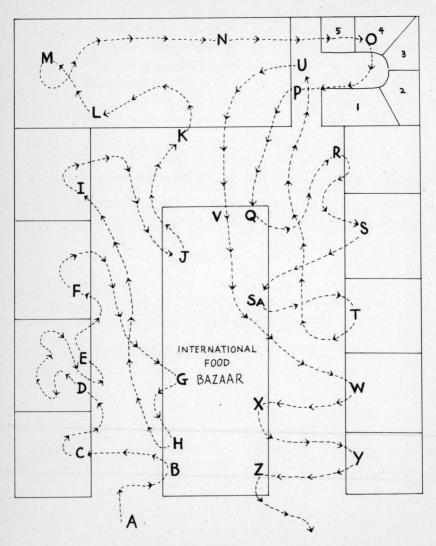

A: Debbie's first stop is the International Food Bazaar for a chocolate-coconut decaf and two of Mrs. Hearth & Home's homemade sticky buns.

B: Debbie spots pink suede outfit in the window of the Sophisticated Lady. Aha! The perfect outfit to wear on her first date with Steve.

C: Enters the shop and purchases the pink suede jacket only—all size 10 skirts are gone.

D: Wanders into Fashion Trends in search of a pink suede skirt. Buys black crepe pants that will fit better after loss of excess water weight.

E: Exits the store, then changes her mind. Reenters and returns the pants for store credit.

F: Walks into Wendy's Victorian Trunk and buys a black merry widow corset.

G: Stops into the International Food Bazaar for a mini-pizza and iced tea.

H: Back to Mrs. Hearth and Home's for a half a dozen sticky buns to take home.

I: Enters Music 4 All and buys Jane Fonda workout tapes.

J: Back to the International Food Bazaar for one last corn dog before beginning new exercise regimen.

K: Next stop is Chasen's Department Store. Snaps up Max Factor's new lip and eye pencils in autumn colors.

L: Tests 43 spray colognes at the perfume counter. Buys a new men's fragrance to keep as a gift for Steve if things work out.

M: Tries on hats and buys one she hates but thinks might go well with pink suede.

N: Wanders through housewares and buys a set of Corelle ware on sale. Slows down in the small appliances aisle, stares blankly at the blenders, and leaves the store.

O: Buys a ticket to *Star Trek V* at Theater Four at 3. Sees Steve go into the theater with Sheila Robinson.

P: Sneaks out of the theater, eating sticky buns en route to the International Food Bazaar.

Q: Consumes three falafels and a large Orange Julius.

R: Enters Ritchie's Shoe Salon and buys spike heels exerting 220 pounds of pressure per square inch.

S: Tries on dirndls at Country Petites and slips into despair when nothing fits.

Sa: Realizes she's in the wrong store. Runs to the Chocolate Pot to celebrate with a Grand Marnier chocolate truffle.

T: Gets a "walk-in" appointment at Scissor Savvy. Asks Serena the stylist for a "new look."

U: Exits Scissor Savvy wearing the new hat and waits for Steve and Sheila to leave the theater—just to be sure it was really them.

V: Inhales large quantities of caramel corn to erase the memory of Steve and Sheila walking out hand in hand.

W: Wanders through the psychology section of the Book Shack.

X: Finds an ice cream cone more psychologically satisfying.

Y: Forgets her parking level and enlists the help of security to find car.

Z: Handsome security guard waits while she gets take-out Chinese.

NOTE: Debbie leaves the mall only to return the next day and return the suede jacket and buy a blender top.

Copping a Premenstrual Plea

Although some crimes of passion have been successfully acquitted with a PMS defense, don't bet on your hormones beating the rap. You just can't blatantly knock over a bakery truck and expect the judge to believe that it was premenstrual instead of premeditated.

Remember! PMS is no excuse for:

▲ illegal dumping of toxic wastes

▲ insider trading

▲ tax evasion

▲ unpaid parking tickets

▲ running a shell game

▲ prostitution

▲ bigamy

▲ fencing stolen fax machines out of your car trunk

▲ counterfeiting

▲ cat burglary

▲ selling arms to the Contras

▲ photocopying copyrighted materials

▲ renting a videotape and rebroadcasting it without the express permission of the licensee

▲ computer hacking

▲ politicking within twenty feet of an election booth

Assault with a Deadly Hormone

It goes without saying that violent or illegal acts do not become a Hostage. However, district attorneys have been known to reduce the charges for certain crimes when it has been proven that the accused had a roaring case of PMS. Ipso facto, "Temporary Insanity by PMS" may come in handy when many of the following crimes against society seem otherwise unjustifiable:

▲ impersonating a food critic

▲ brandishing a butter knife at a Kiwanis pancake breakfast

▲ contributing to the delinquency of a pizza delivery boy

▲ driving under the influence of caffeine

▲ disorderly conduct in a Weight Watchers meeting

▲ assault with intent to kill a hairdresser

▲ lewd and abusive language at a mother-daughter banquet

▲ transporting your neighbor's stereo speakers across state lines

▲ carrying a concealed food processor

I Want to Live, but Not Right Now

Each month, a small percentage of Hostages battle with a hormonal hopelessness so real that the only relief seems to be by ending it all in some revolting way that will make everybody really sorry.

If this sounds familiar, then you know only too well that all you can do is wait it out and remind yourself of reasons to hang in there for another twenty-eight days.

So, just in case your list is running short, let us gently suggest:

▲ *A Few More Reasons to Live*

▲ you can't die and leave your house looking like a pigsty

▲ no one would believe it was only PMS

▲ your husband will dress your remains in something stupid

▲ your children will go through your college diaries and find out about Harold

▲ Estée Lauder is coming out with the spring palette

▲ they're this close to a cure for cellulite (two years away)

▲ Robert Redford is now seeing other women

▲ the lottery jackpot is up to 42 million

▲ Du Pont is working on a wrinkle-free rayon

▲ your gym just hired a masseur

▲ DoveBar Lites just came on the market

▲ next month's *Cosmo* article links chocolate with firm upper arms

▲ you're only six months away from getting that black mark off your credit rating

▲ you're not in any condition to do this correctly

The Mind of the Hormone Hostage

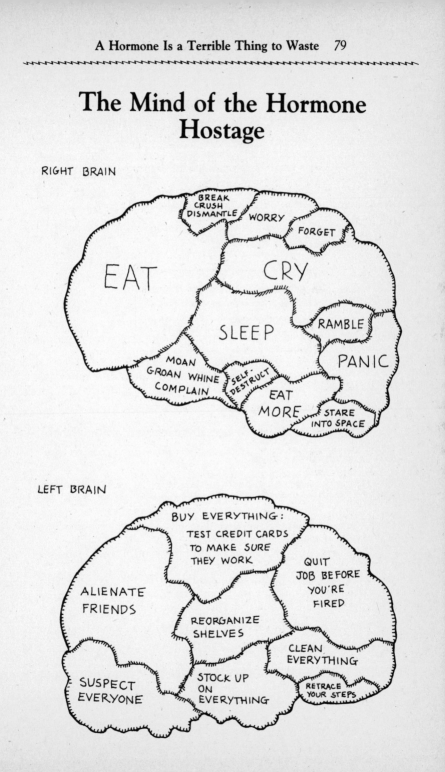

The Gullibility Factor

PMS affects a woman's judgment, which explains why she will buy the wire mesh cocktail dress that the store clerk says makes her look like Cher. A woman's mind is so preoccupied with burning questions such as "Where does my foot go next?" that she does not have the time or energy to challenge statements such as "Semen has no calories." Therefore, always keep this equation in mind:

> The Gullibility Factor in a Hostage rises in direct proportion to the degree of severity of her PMS symptoms.

Learn to recognize these frequently attempted crocks:

"everything you need for a balanced breakfast in one envelope"

"thirty days to thin thighs"

"Smucker's Old-Fashioned Marmalade is a very effective spermicide"

"you're beautiful when you're ovulating"

"I thought watching the game would take your mind off things"

"it's going to cost five hundred bucks just to take it apart and find out what's wrong with it"

"she never gives us homework on weeknights"

"we don't need a piece of paper to say we love each other"

"never needs ironing"

"a smart gal like you will have no problem finding another job"

Easy Quiz #8

BEYOND THE SUBCONSCIOUS HORMONE

Choose the description that most closely fits your first impression of each inkblot below.

Take this test twice—once postmenstrually, and again premenstrually. If the inkblot that looked like a cloud on Day 5 reminds you of heavy artillery on Day 26, beware! PMS is altering more than your waistline! Avoid high-speed amusement rides, Dolby stereo, and mixed drinks with umbrellas in them.

1.
   a. a cloud
   b. a dead bug
   c. a live hand grenade leaving my hand and landing in the rumpus room

2.
   a. two people kissing
   b. steamrolled cat with flea collar
   c. a pizza delivery boy with no underwear

3.
   a. a rose in bloom
   b. a map of Saigon
   c. the bald spot on my boyfriend's head after the kitchen fire

4.
   a. a goose-down pillow
   b. the *Sports Illustrated* swimsuit video with all the tape pulled out like spaghetti
   c. the birthmark on my loan officer's back

5.
   a. tapioca pudding
   b. a pair of dress shields
   c. all my husband's personal effects on the front porch

WOMEN WHO LOVE MEN WHO HATE WOMEN WITH PMS

*In which we deal with matters of the heart vis-à-vis
matters of the hormones. Teaching him to love
that very special part of you can be a truly romantic
way of saying "One of us is changing and it's not going to
be me."*

. . . .

Pat's Story

PMS has always been a part of my life.

My mother had it. Those were the days my father mowed
the lawn, waxed the car, and clipped the hedge until it got dark
and he had to come inside. I can still see him on his Toro, riding
around with a flashlight in his hand.

I could always tell when my big sister was getting her period.
She'd stand on the back porch and argue with her dense boyfriend Derek until Dad would flash the lights and tell Dense
Derek to go home. Then Mary Ann would come inside and
slam doors for an hour.

Most of my girlfriends in college had it. Jeanie would cry,
Peggy would get convinced that people were hiding things from
her, Ava would announce she was "world-weary," and Carol
would spend the day in the snack bar.

I actually thought I'd grow out of PMS someday, but here I
am with a career and a station wagon and a house in the suburbs
and PMS is complicating my life more than ever.

You'd think you'd get used to it. But every month it still comes as a surprise. You say to yourself, "Maybe next month will be different." And a couple of weeks go by and you forget. Good weeks. Weeks when Chris and I want to go to the same movies, when we laugh at the same jokes and make love under the dining room table, when we stay up late and laugh and talk about the future. Three weeks when life is good and I can't imagine deserving such happiness.

Then BANG! It's Day 28 or Day 25 and SHE'S GOT IT AGAIN and suddenly, nothing I say, do, think, want, eat, or wear is right. She doesn't want to go out, she doesn't want to stay in, nothing is funny, we have no future, and the thought of making love under, over, or in anything repels her. For one week, it's like living with someone who needs an exorcist.

Who said men don't suffer from PMS?

of the Lip Can Sink
a Relationship!

Every Hostage knows there are days in the month when all a man has to do is open his mouth and he takes his life in his hands.

Your man must learn that what he says innocently on Monday cannot be said on Thursday without protective headgear and the name of a good lawyer.

Before one wrong word or ill-timed question pushes you over the edge, use this handy guide as a discussion tool or simply tear it out and give it to your loved one to keep in his wallet.

DANGEROUS:	What's for dinner?
SAFER:	Can I help you with dinner?
SAFEST:	Where would you like to go for dinner?
DANGEROUS:	Are you wearing THAT again?
SAFER:	Gee, you look good in brown.
SAFEST:	Wow! Look at you!
DANGEROUS:	What are you so worked up about?
SAFER:	Could we be overreacting?
SAFEST:	Here's fifty dollars.
DANGEROUS:	Should you be eating that?
SAFER:	You know, we've got lots of apples left.
SAFEST:	Can I get you a glass of wine with that?
DANGEROUS:	What did you DO all day?
SAFER:	I hope you didn't overdo today.
SAFEST:	I've always loved you in that robe.

Hormone Heroes

We commend these men who have demonstrated their unique qualifications for relating to the Hormone Hostage:

▲ Merv Griffin
▲ Marvin Mitchelson
▲ Bob Mackie
▲ Ernest and Julio Gallo
▲ Wolfgang Puck
▲ Alan Alda
▲ Richard Simmons
▲ Chef-Boy-Ar-Dee
▲ Robin Leach
▲ C. Everett Koop
▲ Mickey Rooney
▲ Leo Buscaglia

Remember Eva Braun

So, he seems a little insensitive. Maybe he could be more supportive. Maybe you'd swear he only whistles in bed when you're premenstrual. So, the man in your life isn't always the man of your dreams when you're a Hostage nightmare. So what? It could be worse. You could be married to one of these:

▲ Sam Donaldson
▲ Alexander Haig
▲ Norman Mailer
▲ Don King
▲ James Brown
▲ Pee-wee Herman
▲ Sean Penn
▲ Morton Downey, Jr.
▲ Manuel Noriega
▲ Stephen King
▲ Marlon Brando
▲ Claus von Bulow
▲ John McEnroe
▲ Weird Al Yankovic
▲ Bryant Gumbel
▲ Jimmy Swaggart

The Walking Wounded

For every Hormone Hostage, there's an Innocent Bystander shot down in the line of duty.

▲ Sonny Bono

▲ male members of the House of Windsor

▲ Hugh Downs

▲ former lovers of Barbra Streisand

▲ Mike Tyson

Advice to Hearts and Hormones

Q. I've been dating Ralph for six months. Things are going great, but he's starting to notice that "occasionally" I seem to forget our dates, his name, my diaphragm, etc. These are also the same days that I seem to set a lot of accidental fires. I don't want to lose him, but when do I tell what's-his-name that I have terrible PMS?

A. After your name is on his life insurance policies.

Q. What do I say to a man who always makes jokes about my PMS at parties?

A. Ask him if he's heard the one about the Hormone Hostage who flushed her date's keys down the toilet and left early with his best friend?

Q. Every month I experience all the PMS symptoms from Acne to Zoned-out. Will it help if I marry a man who grew up with lots of sisters?

A. Yes, but it will help even more if he grew up with lots of money.

Q. Last night I surprised Susan with a green and black leopard-print teddy with tassels. She took one look and threw it in the fireplace. Does this mean she has PMS?

A. This means she has good taste.

When You Care Enough
to Send the PMS

PMS has a way of complicating even the best of romances. Things are said in the heat of premenstrual passion that can send your man running in the opposite direction. And then, when you try to make amends, you just can't seem to find the right words. Or maybe you can't seem to form them.

Unfortunately, no greeting card has yet managed to capture the spirit of PMS reconciliation. Until now . . .

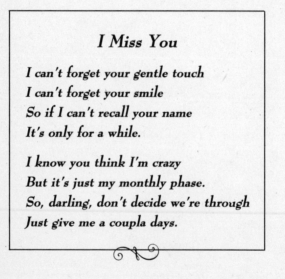

I Miss You

I can't forget your gentle touch
I can't forget your smile
So if I can't recall your name
It's only for a while.

I know you think I'm crazy
But it's just my monthly phase.
So, darling, don't decide we're through
Just give me a coupla days.

Just for You

If we're to have a romance
there's something you should know.
I want to share it with you
Because I love you so.

You can send me to the moon
With just one perfect kiss.
But I'll send you to hell and back
When I have PMS.

♥ ♥ ♥

I'm Sorry

I didn't mean those things I said
about your stupid ties.
I didn't really mean it when
I cut you down to size.

It's just that there are certain days
When I hate everyone.
And taking it all out on you
Makes PMS more fun.

Easy Quiz #9

LOVE ME, LOVE MY HORMONES

Is your man Type I, "Informed," Type I, "Ignorant," Type I, "Inhibited," or Type I, "Insensitive"? See how he measures up in the test below.

1. **Your man comes home to discover you crying in the bathtub with all the water drained out. Does he:**
   a. bring you a cup of herbal tea?
   b. call your mother?
   c. turn around and walk out?
   d. remind you not to use all the hot water?

2. **You and your man have spent five hours shopping for a dress for your class reunion. You've narrowed it down to three dresses but absolutely cannot decide between them. Does he:**
   a. encourage you to buy all three?
   b. ask why you need a new dress anyway?
   c. tell you to meet him in the stereo department when you're done?
   d. mention that they all look too small?

3. **Your breasts are so tender this month that it hurts to walk against the wind. Is your man:**
   a. willing to concentrate on other erogenous zones?
   b. willing to believe that you get as much pleasure "just being close"?
   c. afraid to look at you sideways?
   d. assuring you "I can make them feel better, baby"?

4. **With no evidence, you accuse your man of seeing someone else. Does he:**
   a. cancel his night out with the boys and stay home with you?

b. swear, "I don't want anybody sexy, I just want *you*"?

c. reply, "I wouldn't cheat on you—there's too much disease out there"?

d. say, "If you're talking about Charlene, it didn't mean anything"?

5. There's one piece of Boston cream pie left in the refrigerator. Does he:

a. feed it to the dog and split an apple with you?

b. get you a fork, serve the pie to you on a plate and insist it's just what you needed?

c. eat it himself?

d. eat it in front of you?

K E Y

If you answered "a" to three or more, your man is Type I, "Informed." He knows when to run out for evening-primrose oil and will probably bring back a quart of all-natural, nonfat frozen yogurt at the same time. Supportive, he keeps a record of your cycle in his appointment book.

If you answered "b" to three or more, your man is Type I, "Ignorant." He's as sympathetic as he is baffled. He won't recognize your symptoms on his own, but can be understanding once you explain. This one will pretty much believe anything you tell him.

If you answered "c" to three or more, your man is Type I, "Inhibited." This guy would just plain rather not know. He's the same type that won't show up in the delivery room and probably keeps the lights off during sex. When he hears the word "menstrual," he instinctively crosses his legs.

If you answered "d" to three or more, your man is Type I, "Insensitive." The hormonal antagonist, he sees PMS as another excuse women cooked up to avoid housework. No matter how bad your PMS is, if he gets a paper cut, his pain is worse.

10

THE HORMONE HOSTAGE HOMEMAKER FROM HELL

In which we acknowledge the special needs of the premenstrual mom at home and offer handy household hints suitable for nailing to the refrigerator door.

• • • • • • • • • • • •

Phyllis' Story

One day I discovered my five-year-old girl dressed up in my high heels and best silk dress. It broke my heart to hear little Lisa admonishing her favorite doll: "Mandy! Mother has had it with you! Go play outside for the next two to fourteen days! Now!" It was then I knew that my PMS was getting out of hand. My husband had already moved to the Y, claiming that blood-doping weightlifters were easier to communicate with. A hardly-worth-mentioning misdemeanor had caused me to be dropped from the Junior League roster, and now even my darling Lisa was telling her friends she was adopted. I had to do something before I became alienated from my entire family.

And so, that night as I stood in the pantry arranging boxes of cereal and cake mix according to expiration date, I resolved to seek help.

Hostage Homemaker Handy Hints

In the "can do" tradition of American womanhood, homemakers all across the country are discovering new ways to cope.

Dear Hormone Hostage:

To prevent unhealthful afternoon snacking, I always keep a colorful bowl of fresh fruit for the kids to grab from as they come in from school. This diverts their attention from my stash of Klondike Bars and Eskimo Pies in the freezer. And, it's good for them, too!

Mrs. G.F.
Tulsa, Oklahoma

Dear HH:

Here's how I took care of the red wine stains on my husband's dress shirt last month. I reminded him that nobody drinks red wine anymore, so it must be lipstick. I removed the husband and the shirt followed. Presto! The stain was gone.

Ms. P.K.
Gary, Indiana

Dear HH:

We converted our "Dishes Clean/Dishes Dirty" kitchen magnet into a communication system for our family. Now our reversible magnet reads "Mom's OK/Mom's Got It Bad." This has been a lifesaver!

Mrs. J.R.
New York, New York

Dear HH:

I have a special PMS nightgown. Whenever I wear it, I don't have to say a word. My husband knows it means "I'm not remotely in the mood for anything and you'd be smart to sleep in the den." Month after month, this has saved our marriage.

Mrs. W.P.
Boca Raton, Florida

Here's an interesting twist on the same theme:

Dear HH:

This is my hint for working off premenstrual tension. I save certain household chores for those days when I know I can really do them right! Here's just a few:

distressing and sanding "antique" furniture
beating the Oriental rugs
defrosting the freezer with an ice pick
rehearsing family fire drills
trashing all chipped dishware
snaking the drain

Mrs. H.C.
Pasadena, California

Children of a Lesser Mother

(Caveats for the PMS Mom)

If you are in the throes of PMS, DON'T:

▲ teach your teen-ager to drive

▲ use diaper pins

▲ shop for formals

▲ host the backyard camp-out for Troop 119

▲ make a prom dress

▲ take your teenagers to a Guns n' Roses concert

▲ assemble anything on Christmas Eve

▲ chaperon a field trip

▲ make costumes for the school play

▲ clean out your son's bureau drawers

▲ help your child with any school project that involves flour, water, and salt

Why Mommy Can't Read

Why not turn precious moments of quality time with your children into learning opportunities? Simply adapt their favorite stories to introduce your little ones to PMS and help them recognize your erratic behavior as natural and fun. Kids will love it when you improvise and turn a familiar tale into a timely fable such as this:

Snow White

*nce upon a time, probably last month and most likely next month too, a beautiful Queen asked her mirror, "Who is the fairest of them all?" The mirror answered, "Snow White, because she's kinder and gentler." The Queen, who otherwise would have been merely annoyed, was experiencing premenstrual headaches and severe water weight gain and became enraged, sort of like when Mommy yells for no reason at all.*

The paranoid Queen sent Snow White into the forest, knowing that the girl would never find her way back because Snow White had no sense of direction during that time of the month.

After wandering aimlessly, conversing with flora and fauna and strange premenstrual voices, Snow happened upon a quaint cottage. Finding it empty, she made a beeline for the refrigerator and consumed everything that wasn't plastic or glass. Struck by a sudden domestic urge, she compulsively began to tidy up, rearranging the furniture as she went and complaining because nobody was around to help out. Finally exhausted, she lay across seven tiny beds and dreamed of short men who are easily dominated.

Before long, she was rudely awakened by the happy, hearty sound of males who don't have anything better to do than whistle on their way home from work. "Shut up!" she screamed. "I'm here now and your lives are changed forever." The seven cowering dwarfs obediently fell into line and introduced themselves: Cranky, Weepy, Clumsy, Messy, Puffy, Hungry, and Dick. "I think I'm going to feel right at home here," said Snow White.

She lived there with the seven dwarfs until one day she realized in her innermost being that something primal was missing in her life— something that Mommy doesn't think you're old enough to learn about yet.

It depressed her so much that she started binging on apples and finally got hold of a bad one. She fell into a deathlike coma, just like when Mommy wants to be alone sometimes.

The seven dwarfs returned home that night to discover Snow White sprawled on the floor. Assuming that she was just dealing with a severe hormonal drop, they left her alone until a handsome gynecologist came along on his horse and recognized her symptoms. Being a real prince, he gave her a lift out of the forest and a prescription for progesterone therapy.

They fell in love, of course, and got married, and they all lived in reasonable happiness three weeks out of every month until the prince had had enough and took her back to the forest to live with the dwarfs.

THE END

Other Domestic Fables for Our Time

With a little ingenuity, you can adapt practically any favorite children's book to gently communicate to your little one how Mommy's feeling today. Here are just a few:

▲ **Curious George Gets Shot**

▲ **The Bitch Who Stole Christmas**

▲ **The Care Bears Burn in Hell**

▲ **The Little Engine That Didn't Give a Damn**

▲ **The Incredibly Messy House at Pooh Corner**

▲ **Sleeping Ugly**

▲ **Charlotte's Web of Desire**

▲ **Ask Me a Riddle and I'll Kill You**

▲ **Free to Be You, but Not Around Me**

▲ **Nancy Drew and the Mystery of Prescription Drugs**

That Was No Lady, That Was My Mother
(A Note to the Children of Hormone Hostages)

In the life of every child there inevitably comes the awful realization that one's mother does not exist solely to tie one's laces and to reach those forbidden things on top of the refrigerator. She is a separate individual, unique and fallible, capable of accidentally breaking windows and china and stuff, crying hysterically, and doing things she doesn't have any good excuse for, *just like you!*

Here's a list of warning signs to help you recognize when to be extra-good boys and girls. If more than five of the following occur on any single day, you may be more comfortable in a shelter. See your school nurse or trusted adult friend, such as a minister or school counselor. Older children may want to investigate summer camp, foreign exchange, or early enlistment.

Mommy's PMS Primer
(Survival Tips for the Crayola Set)

Stay away from Mommy when:

1. It's noon and she's still in her robe.
2. She keeps calling you by your brother's name.
3. You can stay at Susie's as long as you want.
4. It's four and she's still in her robe.
5. She cries and lets you wear dirty clothes.
6. The mailman is still there when you get home from school.
7. She gives your pets away.
8. She forgets to pick you up at school.
9. She eats all your Halloween candy.
10. You're allowed to take a bath for two hours and forty-five minutes.
11. Daddy works late.

Easy Quiz #10

HOME IS WHERE YOUR HORMONES ARE

In the examples below, circle the word in each group that does not belong with the others. Example: a. spring cleaning; b. dry cleaning; c. self-cleaning; d. four-star hotel. Answer: d.

1. a. Pamprin
   b. Motrin
   c. Midol
   d. Old Grand-Dad

2. a. Formula 409
   b. Heinz 57
   c. Vicks Formula 44
   d. AK-47

3. a. whole grain
   b. long grain
   c. ten grain
   d. migraine

4. a. husband
   b. father
   c. lover
   d. pizza delivery boy

5. a. car pool
   b. car wash
   c. car seat
   d. Cartier

6. a. calcium
   b. magnesium
   c. iron
   d. Milk Duds

7. a. suicide
   b. homicide
   c. genocide
   d. spermicide

K E Y

If you failed to circle "d" for your answer to each question, you are most likely a Hostage Homemaker. In the days prior to your period, it is recommended that you remain indoors and avoid operating anything with a cord.

11
THE HORMONE
HOSTAGE ON
CAMPUS

In which the Hostage Coed enrolls in PMS 101. An intensive course in making the premenstrual grade for which there is no prerequisite other than a demonstrated desire to graduate without killing, disabling, or otherwise alienating yourself and others.

• • • • • • • • • • • •

Courtney's Story

Every twenty-eight days, I do one of three things: change my major, change my roommate, apply to another school. College is supposed to be the best years of my life, but then so was high school, and junior high. Come to think of it, I haven't had a good time since puberty.

If only I could be like all the other girls. Popular, fun-loving, and menstrually cool. Instead, I've spent the last two years desperately trying to fit in, transferring from college to college. I was a freshman at Ohio State and transferred mid-semester to NYU to be near better restaurants.

I spent spring break at Fort Lauderdale, took a wrong turn, and ended the term at SMU. Every girl there had been Miss Dallas, Miss El Paso, Miss Houston, or Miss Nacogdoches. Nobody had even heard of PMS, and if any one of them had menstruated, they wouldn't admit it.

After that, I bounced from school to school. I liked the University of Alaska, but still got hot flashes. I did okay at Arizona State, but still retained water. UCLA was supposed to be a party school, but I still hated everybody. I finally sought academic retreat at Holy Cross, where I was expelled for physically threatening the bell tower monitor three days before my period.

Now I'm awaiting acceptance letters from Cal Tech, the Barbizon modeling school, and Debbie Dootson's Truck Driving Institute. I guess my chances of being a normal college coed are over, let alone my dream of ever becoming White House Chief of Staff.

Don'ts for the Campus Hostage

If you won't listen to your parents, at least listen to us! When it's PMS time in the quad, NEVER:

▲ enter the Sophomore Beer-Chugging Contest

▲ dissect

▲ discuss your failing grades with that cute professor whose marriage is on the rocks

▲ be a subject in your boyfriend's Psychology 101 project

▲ star in any Experimental Theater production

▲ attend any class discussing Nietzsche

▲ sign up for any course with the word "Advanced" in the title

▲ switch your major from English to Organic Chem

▲ seduce a freshman from the Midwest

▲ cook in your room

▲ be the top of the cheerleaders' pyramid

▲ volunteer to be a Flag Team substitute

▲ schedule your personal interview for a Rhodes scholarship

▲ get a six-dollar make-over at the School of Cosmetology

▲ invite any team back to your room for a victory toast

▲ become a Big Sister

▲ date anyone whose fraternity nickname is "Anaconda"

▲ enter the downhill freestyle at Winter Carnival

Phi Mu Sigma

It's tough enough to go to college these days and survive courses like "Perceptual Psychophysics" and "Microeconomics in a Macro World." You also must leave home and adjust to a new living environment where you have to make your own bed and pay for your own ibuprofen and nobody understands why once a month you skip volleyball practice, stay in your room, and beat the stuffing out of Binky the Bear.

But hormonal housing and support are finally available to desperate dorm dwellers. A fledgling sorority is founding chapters in colleges and universities all over the country, providing loving sisterhood for misunderstood Hostage Coeds in need of social and academic acceptance:

Phi Mu Sigma

▲ *MOTTO*

Damnant Quod Non Intelligunt
("they condemn what they do not understand")

▲ *FLOWER*

the snapdragon (stands for creativity and senseless violence)

▲ *COLORS*

Chocolate Brown and Indecisive Blue

▲ *RUSH WEEK*

You will be considered for membership after completion of the following:

1. Written recommendations attesting to your PMS symptoms from:

   a doctor who has treated you for at least two of the following: colic, measles, acne, hot flashes

   a teacher who is familiar with your strengths, weaknesses, and tendency to forget your locker combination

   a personal friend of at least three years who has seen you gain ten or more pounds within thirty-six hours

2. Scavenger hunt. You will be given two hours to find these items:

   a good-tasting, sugar-free brownie

   a nonalcoholic wine that still gives you a buzz

   a senior male who thinks premenstrual syndrome is sexy

   a senior girl who has never used diuretics

   an ovulating professor in pajamas

3. While premenstrual, you must find your way back to the PMS House from an undisclosed location in less than fourteen days.

4. For one week, you must wear a T-shirt to classes, meals, and all campus functions that reads: AFFECT DOESN'T PMS ME.

▲ *HOUSE RULES*

1. You must maintain either a GPA of 3.0 or a weight limit of 150 lbs.

2. All take-out food delivered to the PMS House must be enough for everyone.

3. No two persons whose PMS cycles coincide shall share a room, bathroom, or boyfriend.

▲ *CANDLE LIGHTING*

This traditional secret ceremony of light and ritual is held whenever a PMS sister becomes engaged (or when she has dated the same guy for three consecutive cycles).

▲ *THE PHI MU SIGMA PIN*

To prevent unnecessary injury and to protect fine cashmere, the striking symbol of Phi Mu Sigma has been designed with a Velcro backing.

Onward, Hostage Sisters
(to the tune of "Onward, Christian Soldiers")

Onward, Hostage Sisters
We've Got PMS!
What we're marching for is
Anybody's guess!

We can't fold the ban-ner
We can't step in time
We can't bear to hear the drums
Or make this anthem rhyme right

Onward, Hostage Sisters
Hold our hormones high
Marching into battle
Gee, I hope there's pie!

▲ *SONGS*

As Months Go By
(sung to the tune of "As Time Goes By")

My life is just a mess
'Cause I've got PMS
But you won't see me cry
On Phi Mu Sisters I rely
As months go by

And when my ankles swell
It's really hard to tell
If I should live or die
I leave it up to Phi Mu Sigma
As months go by

Hormones and migraines,
Never get a break
Anxious and angry
Men think I'm a flake
What do I care?
I need a chocolate shake
On that I can rely

It's still the same old menses
I just can't comprehend these
Cycles if I try
But Phi Mu Sigma understands me
As months go by

Easy Quiz #11

TAKING THE PMAT—"THE PREMENSTRUAL APTITUDE TEST"

You have five minutes to complete the following exam. Be sure to use a No. 2 pencil and keep your eyes on your own work. If you finish before time is up, go back, check your answers, and spend the remaining time wondering why you have to use a No. 2 pencil.

▲ Computational

1. If Marsha retains water at a rate of 200 milliliters per Diet Crush, how many 12-ounce cans must she consume before she no longer fits into that acid-washed denim miniskirt she borrowed from Jennifer and forgot to return until after Jennifer got pregnant and dropped out?

2. If Candace ovulates every 29.6 days (x) and her PMS symptoms (y) occur three days before and two days after her period each month, how many weekends per quarter can she safely spend with Ted at Amherst? Show your work.

▲ Logic Problems

In each example, choose the answer that most accurately completes the statement given.

1. Salt is to bloat what chocolate is to _____.
   a. acne
   b. sexual fulfillment
   c. die for
   d. all of the above
   e. none of the above

2. Homecoming is to fall what _____ is to month.
   a. menstruation
   b. ovulation

c. money from Dad
d. all of the above
e. (a) and (b)
f. (a) and (c)

▲ *Comprehension*

Read each paragraph carefully before answering questions.

1. Gary is Heather's brother. Heather has slept with three of Gary's roommates this semester. One is Gary's best friend. Heather sleeps with all of Gary's best friends. One is from Nebraska. Will Heather's child have farming instincts? (YES) (NO) (NOT ENOUGH INFORMATION) (DON'T CARE)

2. "According to some sources, ninety percent of all women experience some form of premenstrual syndrome during their childbearing years. Symptoms can be as simple as cramping and fatigue or so severe as to be incapacitating (or so they say). Because the symptoms vary so widely from month to month and from woman to woman, diagnosis is difficult and casts doubt on the existence of PMS at all, suggesting instead a form of mass hysteria."

Mark the statements below that apply to the paragraph you have just read:

    a. From the tone of this passage, we can assume that it was written by a man.
    b. Ninety percent is a low figure.
    c. Who says cramping and fatigue are simple?

STOP! Put your pencil down and tell the proctor you're ready for a nap.

12

THE HORMONE HOSTAGE ON HER OWN

In which the single Hostage learns to fly solo with her hormonal ups and downs and discovers that being a bitch without a witness is probably a blessing in disguise.

• • • • • • • • • • • • •

Donna's Story

I'm twenty-nine, single, considered attractive and have a good job. I have lots of friends, a great condo at the marina and an 800 number. Everybody thinks my life is perfect. But I keep a terrible secret that prevents me from truly getting close to anyone. Every month for six or seven days I'm overcome with strong maternal urges. I cry every time I see a Gerber baby. I read storybooks aloud to my dog. I've learned to crochet and I'm the only childless woman in La Leche League. I can handle the usual PMS, but this monthly maternal madness could ruin my date life. Last week, the guy I'm seeing caught a glimpse of the Kindergym in my guest room and said goodnight at nine fifteen. Help!

Single but Not Alone

Donna's story is a familiar one. In addition to the usual symptoms, the single Hormone Hostage may experience an increased need for companionship—from a husband, a baby, a boyfriend, a roommate, or even the man who comes to check the meter. In a time when everyone seems to be pairing and cocooning, it's hard to be single and just this side of schizophrenic. Someone should tell Donna to lighten up. She needs an endocrinologist, not an obstetrician.

I've Got a Right
to Scream the Blues

To the single Hormone Hostage, being unmarried and hormonally unsound is a mixed blessing. Circumstances that can seem unnaturally cruel premenstrually can have their advantages in the postmenstrual light of day.

So remember, when the hormones are running high, it doesn't do you any good to dwell on the fact that you feel undesirable, unloved, and unattractive, and worst of all, that there is:

▲ no one to ask if he hears that ringing sound too

▲ no one to wake up and keep you company when you have insomnia

▲ no one at home to call to see if you left the curling iron on

▲ no one with a second income to help cover the absolutely essential purchase of a tanning bed

▲ no one to talk you out of getting a nose job

▲ no one to bring your purse to the supermarket when you're standing at the checkout counter with no money and six bags of Doritos and bean dip

▲ no one to intercept those phone calls from your mother on the days her PMS is worse than yours

▲ no one to tell you that your eggplant linguini is actually pretty edible

▲ no one to talk you out of the bathroom on Monday morning

▲ no one to pry you out of the leather skirt you had no business wearing this week anyway

▲ no one to scream at irrationally and blame for your general discontentment with a life void of meaning

Caveats for the Unmarried PMS Victim

When stricken with severe symptoms, you should never:

▲ get anything monogrammed

▲ stop in to talk to the Army recruiter

▲ say "I love you" with your eyes closed

▲ attend a wedding

▲ take the results of a *Cosmo* quiz seriously

▲ take your nephews to the zoo

▲ call up old boyfriends

▲ try new forms of birth control

▲ change your own oil

▲ answer a personal ad from any man living in Alaska

▲ lunch with married girlfriends

▲ wear fishnet stockings

▲ go on a National Audubon Society Singles Hike

▲ become a surrogate mother

▲ choose a china pattern

▲ meet his children

▲ sleep with an evangelist

▲ read to your date aloud from your journal

▲ give yourself a bikini wax

▲ cancel a blind date (if he likes you now, this could be forever)

▲ become a prison pen pal

▲ reconsider marrying your cousin

Full Refrigerator and Empty Arms

(Better Things to Do than Sit at Home and Wallow in Self-Pity, Your Symptoms, or Your Bathtub)

▲ date that pathetic guy who's been asking you out for months

▲ organize your hosiery drawer

▲ memorize all the teams and player rosters in the NFL

▲ buy emergency road flares

▲ vacation with a gay male friend

▲ send old love letters to their new wives

▲ pawn jewelry from old lovers

▲ buy an off-road vehicle and practice at home

Tracking the Perfect PMS Mate

Good looks and money don't necessarily qualify him to be your perfect helpmate. Stamina, patience, and a sense of humor are essential qualities in the Hostage Hubby. So are the following:

▲ Boy Scout merit badges in animal husbandry and CPR

▲ raised by a mother, two aunts, and three sisters (preferably, all of whom reside in a different country now)

▲ graduate of Cordon Bleu

▲ close personal relationship with his Creator

▲ good rapport with his personal banker

▲ recognizes the long-term value of always purchasing designer clothes

▲ owns multiple residences

▲ has no political aspirations

▲ understands the necessity of two bathrooms

▲ travels several weeks out of the month

▲ once competed as an Ironman Triathlete

Looking for Love in All the Right Professions

It takes a special kind of fella to love a Hostage. And an even more special one to take her for better or worse, all twenty-eight to thirty-one days out of every month. That venture capitalist or foreign diplomat may look good to you now, but when you're having one of those days, you may wish you were married to one of these instead:

▲ dermatologist   ▲ criminal lawyer

▲ dry cleaner   ▲ makeup artist

▲ locksmith   ▲ florist

▲ physical therapist   ▲ confectioner

▲ plumber   ▲ mentalist

Easy Quiz #12
"ARE YOU BETTER OFF SINGLE?"

Some of us have enough trouble living with our hormones, let alone living with a man too. Don't imagine that having a man around will necessarily take your mind off your PMS problems.

Of course, your hormones won't pay half the rent, but maybe they're the only roommate some Hostages should have.

▲ Circle "T" or "F":

1. I will not go out on a date the week before my period. (T) or (F)

2. I feel most comfortable referring to PMS as a "female problem." (T) or (F)

3. I am most likely to reveal my sexual history to a new man ten days before my period.   (T) or (F)

4. Confusing men with my PMS makes me feel superior. (T) or (F)

5. I am convinced that PMS comes from picking up someone's Jockey shorts off the floor.   (T) or (F)

6. PMS is a punishment from God for my past sexual behavior. (T) or (F)

7. I don't need a husband to have a child.   (T) or (F)

8. I have my carpets shampooed every other Thursday.   (T) or (F)

9. No one must ever see me naked.   (T) or (F)

10. There is no place in my life for joint checking accounts or televised sports.   (T) or (F)

11. I have always spent the holidays with all twenty-six members of my family and I always will.   (T) or (F)

12. I don't see anything funny about this book.   (T) or (F)

K E Y

If you answered "T" to six or more of the statements above, chances are that you have some unresolved problems. You probably never learned to share in kindergarten and you were the last girl to take a shower in junior high gym class. You would be wise to avoid rushing into marriage and start out living with something simple, like a ficus tree.

13
PMS and Proud

In which we proudly unite as a body (albeit a water-bloated one) to transform ourselves, to effect social change, and to become yet another grossly misunderstood special interest group.

• • • • • • • • • • • •

Gloria's Story

I spent the first twenty-five years of my life thinking I had more moods than Mantovani. Then I spent the next ten years realizing it was only PMS. Only PMS? Yes. It's a rotten inconvenience at the least and the best excuse for self-immolation at its worst. But it's only PMS, it's not cancer or herpes, or a six-year audit by the IRS. I've learned to live with it. I can control it now with vitamins and good food and a lot of physical violence to simulated wood furniture. Month after month, I can plan on it coming, which is more than I can say for my husband. And when people give me that familiar "what's your problem?" glare, I just stick out my pimpled chin, toss back my dull, lifeless hair, stand confidently on my own two swollen feet, and proclaim: "I have PMS and I'm damned proud!"

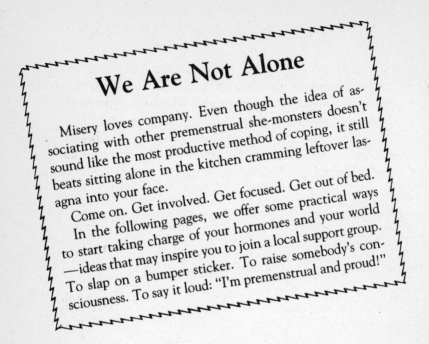

We Are Not Alone

Misery loves company. Even though the idea of associating with other premenstrual she-monsters doesn't sound like the most productive method of coping, it still beats sitting alone in the kitchen cramming leftover lasagna into your face.

Come on. Get involved. Get focused. Get out of bed. In the following pages, we offer some practical ways to start taking charge of your hormones and your world —ideas that may inspire you to join a local support group. To slap on a bumper sticker. To raise somebody's consciousness. To say it loud: "I'm premenstrual and proud!"

Hostages Helping Hostages

PMS knows no borders. All across the nation, independent support groups are sprouting up to provide Hostages with mutual nurturing, loving acceptance, and scheduled opportunities for communal feeding frenzies.

It may be difficult at first to share your hormonal horrors with a room full of ovulating strangers. But remember, you may feel like a human volcano, but no woman is an island. Never underestimate the power of a room full of women in flux!

▲ *National Organizations*

PMS Without Partners
Los Angeles, Chicago, New York

Mothers Against Ovulation
headquarters: Boston, Massachusetts

PRISONS—PRemenstrual Inmates
Stressed Out by Neurotic Symptoms
national correspondence
organization
headquarters: Women's Cellblock,
State Prison
Canon City, Colorado

POOR S.O.B.S—Premenstrual
Organization Of
Recuperating Significant Others,
Boyfriends, and Spouses
headquarters: Hartford, Connecticut

Big, Beautiful PMS Sufferers
headquarters: New York, New York

▲ *Regional Support Groups*

West

Sisters on the Faultline
Los Angeles, California
meets every Saturday morning
Benny's Floating Deli Barge
Santa Monica Pier 9:30 A.M.

Water Retainers of the Southwest
Albuquerque, New Mexico
meets Mondays, Wednesdays,
Fridays
Maria's Pizza TeePee
(drop-ins welcome)
noon and 6 P.M.

Women Who Sew Too Much
Cedar Hills, Utah
meets Saturdays
Levi's State Border Bowl 'N' Brew
Alamosa, Colorado
8 P.M.

*Holiday Hormone Hostage
Extravaganza de Paris on Ice!*
Las Vegas, Nevada
(showgirls only, please)
contact: Castrina Menarche,
Caesar's Palace, after 4 A.M.

Northwest

Boise Hot Flash Society
Boise, Idaho
meets every other Thursday
U-Stuffit Spud Den
7:30 P.M.

Disoriented Daughters of the Tundra
Juneau, Kodiak, Nome, and parts
north, Alaska
party line Sunday nights 6 P.M.–
midnight

Midwest

Grim Reapers of Central Illinois
Centralia, Illinois
meets Wednesdays
Chez Centralia—Boulangerie, Gas,
and Trout Pond
6:30 P.M.

Dairy Queens Anonymous
Sheboygan, Wisconsin
meets Tuesday evenings
Smorgy Boy (on Harper)
sundown

Nail Biters of the Alamo

San Antonio, Texas
meets every other Friday
Yellow Rose Fitness Emporium &
Grille
(bring your own meat)
6 P.M.

South

Grits and Bear It—PMS Support Circle

Mobile, Alabama
meets mornings, Monday–Friday
Clydene's Home of the Big Biscuit
dawn

Hostage Travelers Aid

Orlando, Florida
PMS Pavilion, Epcot Center
open daily 8 A.M.–closing
(don't miss "Voyage Through
Linda's Fallopian Tubes"—tours
leave on the half hour)

Mid-Atlantic

League of Young Executives With TBS (Tender Breast Syndrome)

Washington, D.C.
monthly luncheon
The Endometraeum (members only)

Northeast

Cyclical Shoppers of Long Island

Hewlett, New York
meets every afternoon and Thursday
nights
"Frogasm" Frozen Yogurt Shoppe
Five Towns Mall, Hempstead

Back Bay Scrod and Chocolate Cravers

Boston, Massachusetts
meets Monday nights
Monaghan's Hand-Dipt Delicacies
7–10 P.M.

Hormone Hostage on Board!

Like every other important issue in America, PMS belongs on your bumper. So, demonstrate your Hostage spirit and share your PMS pride by displaying any one of these personal messages wherever you go:

ARE WE OVULATING YET?

ANOTHER MOTHER WITH PMS

PMS—YOUR DIVINE RIGHT

WHERE AM I DRIVING? CALL 1-800-PMS-LOST

ALL WE ARE SAYING IS GIVE PMS A CHANCE

HORMONE HOSTAGES DO IT EVERY 28 DAYS

HONK IF YOU'RE RETAINING WATER

I BRAKE FOR ESTROGEN

Hormone Hostage International

▲ *Welcome New Members!*

If you're like millions of other women with PMS, sooner or later you've had to terminate your membership in any number of organizations. Or it's been terminated for you. Maybe you forgot to pay your dues. Maybe you stood up at the last general meeting and screamed that everyone was looking at you funny and you hated wearing those stupid name tags and why aren't there better refreshments?

Whatever the little reasons, the big reason you can't stay committed to anything civic, fraternal, or charitable is that it meets monthly, and so do your hormones.

Well, here's one organization that won't let you go. Hormone Hostage International is a worldwide association of premenstrual women who understand that you can't bring the cookies to the next meeting because you'll either forget or eat them all in the car on the way.

THIS CERTIFIES THAT

_____

MEMBER SINCE:

_____

IS A MEMBER IN GOOD STANDING OF HORMONE HOSTAGE INTERNATIONAL AND AS A LIVING EXAMPLE OF PREMENSTRUAL SYNDROME

MEMBERSHIP CATEGORY:

ACTIVE _____

INACTIVE _____

IMMOBILE _____

IS HEREBY ENTITLED TO EXHIBIT PHYSICAL, MENTAL, AND EMOTIONAL FLUCTUATIONS WITHOUT TAKING ANY CRAP FROM YOU.

HORMONE HOSTAGE EMERGENCY INFO:

BAIL BONDSMAN: _____

PIZZA DELIVERY: _____

24-HOUR MINI MARKET: _____

NEXT OF KIN: _____

Hormone Hostage Alert
ID Bracelet

You're in an elevator and you suddenly panic. You can't decide between UP, DOWN, or PULL THIS LEVER. A motorcycle cop stops you to mention you've been dragging a Siamese cat for three blocks and you stare at him uncomprehendingly. They pull you kicking and screaming out of Hallmark Cards after you savagely rip up the "Special Moments" section.

You're in trouble and nobody understands. What WILL you do?

Don't be caught with your hormones down. If you can't explain it, let your Hostage Alert bracelet say it for you. The following models available in gold, sterling silver, stainless steel, and licorice.

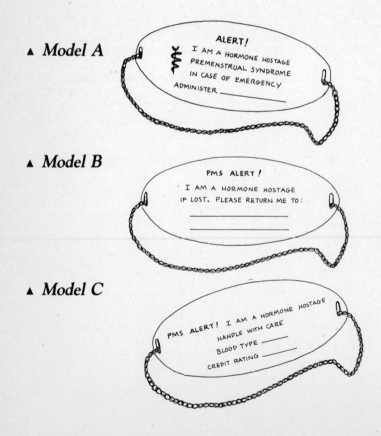

▲ *Model A*

ALERT!
I AM A HORMONE HOSTAGE
PREMENSTRUAL SYNDROME
IN CASE OF EMERGENCY
ADMINISTER _____

▲ *Model B*

PMS ALERT!
I AM A HORMONE HOSTAGE
IF LOST, PLEASE RETURN ME TO:
_____
_____

▲ *Model C*

PMS ALERT! I AM A HORMONE HOSTAGE
HANDLE WITH CARE
BLOOD TYPE _____
CREDIT RATING _____

Suggested Reading

Bloom, Penne. "PMS and the Deep Pan Pizza Phenomenon." *Journal of the Fast Food Industry Council* 37 (Fall 1987): 22–29.

Adams, Welles V., M.D., M.B.A. *Cashing In: Financing Your Premenstrual Shopping Sprees Through Real Estate Leveraging.* New York: Wethersfield Press, 1988.

Darling, B. Jean, and Betty L. Rogers. *How Then Shall We Ovulate? A Biblical Approach to PMS.* Dallas: Dovetail Books, 1986.

Garzilli, R.D. "PMS and the Plea Bargaining Process: The Murphy Bed Murders—A Case Study." *New England Law and Hormones Review* 36 (1954): 12–22.

Fuchs, Betty. *I Was the Mother of the Premenstrual Bride.* New York: Something Blue Press, 1987.

Hiroshi, Miyako. *TokyoRobics: Shinto Hostage Sisters Share Their Shape-Up Secrets.* Tokyo: Kasukabe Publishing, 1988.

Fisher, Robert. *The Icewoman Cometh: A Man's Perspective on PMS.* New York: Virility House, 1988.

Rhodes, Warner J. "Gridlock and the Incidence of PMS Perpetrators." *Traffic Cop Quarterly* 139 (Fall 1985): 56–57.

Witte, Mary. *Cooking Without Knives: Planning Your PMS Menus.* Salt Lake City: Pinecliffe Press, 1989.

Wollenscraft, Lois. *The Quick and Easy Men- and Water-Loss Manual.* New York: Amphibian Publications, 1988.

The Hostage's Creed

I BELIEVE:

that premenstrual syndrome really does exist and anyone who says it doesn't should be shot,

&~

that my mood swings and occasional use of diuretics are only parts of the whole that is I and do not define the postmenstrual woman that is Me,

&~

that just because I don't always make sense doesn't mean I don't know what's going on,

&~

that regular sugar binges and insatiable demands for high- and low-quality chocolate products will not significantly affect global food supplies,

&~

that the glands that rule the hormones rock the world,

&~

that what does not destroy me only makes me more difficult to live with,

&~

that through education and honest, open dialogue we can promote understanding between the nations but it will have absolutely no impact on my skin problems,

&~

and that the Creator of all things has some serious explaining to do.

&~

Bibliography

• • • • • • • • • • • • •

Dalton, Katharina. *Once a Month: The Original Premenstrual Syndrome Handbook*. Claremont, California: Hunter House, 1979.

Harrison, Michelle. *Self-help for Premenstrual Syndrome*. New York: Random House, 1982.

Lark, Susan, M.D. *Premenstrual Syndrome Self-Help Book*. Los Altos, California: PMS Self-Help Center, 1984.

Lauersen, Niels, and Eileen Stukane. *Listen to Your Body*. New York: Simon & Schuster, 1982.

———. *PMS: Premenstrual Syndrome and You; Next Month Can Be Different*. New York: Simon & Schuster, Inc., 1983.

About the Authors

• • • • • • • • • • • • •

Martha Williamson and Robin Sheets met in Pasadena, California, where, as struggling coworkers in a nonprofit organization, they discovered that $1.50 could get them a full meal off any Happy Hour hors d'oeuvres table in town.

Raging Hormones marks the high point of a friendship based on tolerance, humor, and a mutual dedication to helping Hormone Hostages around the world find peace, support, and designer shoes at bargain prices.

The two women have been friends for twelve years and since 1983 their menstrual cycles have coincided with uncanny accuracy.

Martha Williamson is single and seems incapable of maintaining a relationship for more than twenty-eight days.

Born and raised in Denver, Colorado, Martha graduated from Williams College in Massachusetts, despite consuming eight boxes of Raisinets and getting lost on her way to the podium at commencement.

Now a resident of Los Angeles, Martha's current interests include returning phone calls, hiking nowhere in particular, crying in public for no apparent reason, and singing torch songs in piano bars with poor lighting.

In her other identity as a writer/producer for network television, Martha points proudly to the fact that she has never won an Emmy for something she didn't write. Her credits include numerous variety specials and situation comedies, most recently NBC's "The Facts of Life," "Raising Miranda" for CBS, and ABC-TV's "Living Dolls."

Robin Sheets was born and raised in the San Fernando Valley. She graduated from Azusa Pacific University and spent ten years as a public relations consultant because it allowed her to stay home a lot and work in her nightgown.

She became Director of Marketing Communications for a national charity when she recognized in herself a deep need for a meaningful life's work and a comprehensive dental plan.

In 1988, Sheets was selected as one of Five Outstanding Californians by the California Jaycees. She has received numerous other awards for community service, but the one she treasures most is the Distinguished Friend Trophy awarded in 1986 at great personal expense by her coauthor Martha Williamson, a friend for twelve years (that's 144 in PMS years).

Robin resides in Pasadena, California, with her husband John and their dogs Deacon and Satin Sheets.